THE PEARL

OTHER TITLES IN THE GREENHAVEN PRESS LITERARY COMPANION SERIES:

AMERICAN AUTHORS

Maya Angelou
Stephen Crane
Emily Dickinson
William Faulkner
F. Scott Fitzgerald
Nathaniel Hawthorne
Ernest Hemingway
Herman Melville
Arthur Miller
Eugene O'Neill
Edgar Allan Poe
John Steinbeck
Mark Twain
Thornton Wilder

AMERICAN LITERATURE

The Adventures of
  Huckleberry Finn
The Adventures of Tom
  Sawyer
The Call of the Wild
The Catcher in the Rye
The Crucible
Death of a Salesman
The Glass Menagerie
The Grapes of Wrath
The Great Gatsby
Of Mice and Men
The Old Man and the Sea
The Scarlet Letter
A Separate Peace

BRITISH AUTHORS

Jane Austen
Joseph Conrad
Charles Dickens

BRITISH LITERATURE

Animal Farm
The Canterbury Tales
Great Expectations
Hamlet
Julius Caesar
Lord of the Flies
Macbeth
Pride and Prejudice
Romeo and Juliet
Shakespeare: The Comedies
Shakespeare: The Histories
Shakespeare: The Sonnets
Shakespeare: The Tragedies
A Tale of Two Cities
Wuthering Heights

WORLD AUTHORS

Fyodor Dostoyevsky
Homer
Sophocles

WORLD LITERATURE

All Quiet on the Western
  Front
The Diary of a Young Girl
A Doll's House

THE GREENHAVEN PRESS

Literary Companion

TO AMERICAN LITERATURE

READINGS ON

THE PEARL

David Bender, *Publisher*
Bruno Leone, *Executive Editor*
Bonnie Szumski, *Series Editor*
Jill Karson, *Book Editor*

Greenhaven Press, San Diego, CA

Every effort has been made to trace the owners of copyrighted material. The articles in this volume may have been edited for content, length, and/or reading level. The titles have been changed to enhance the editorial purpose. Those interested in locating the original source will find the complete citation on the first page of each article.

Library of Congress Cataloging-in-Publication Data

Readings on The pearl / Jill Karson, book editor.
      p.   cm. — (The Greenhaven Press literary companion to American literature)
    Includes bibliographical references and index.
    ISBN 1-56510-854-X (pbk. : alk. paper). —
ISBN 1-56510-855-8 (lib. bdg. : alk. paper)
    1. Steinbeck, John, 1902–1968. Pearl. 2. Avarice in literature. I. Karson, Jill. II. Series.
PS3537.T3234P496   1999
813'.52—dc21   98-21204
                                              CIP

Cover photo: Sonya Noskowiak, courtesy of Arthur F. Noskowiak, The John Steinbeck Collection, Stanford University Libraries.

Copyright ©1999 by Greenhaven Press, Inc.
PO Box 289009
San Diego, CA 92198-9009
Printed in the U.S.A.

If this story is a parable, perhaps everyone takes his own meaning from it and reads his own life into it.

John Steinbeck,
epigraph to The Pearl

CONTENTS

Foreword   9

Introduction   11

John Steinbeck: A Biography   13

Chapter 1: Important Themes in *The Pearl*

1. The Nature of Good and Evil in *The Pearl*
by Michael J. Meyer   29

Steinbeck invests *The Pearl* with a moral lesson about good
and evil; specifically, that good and evil are intertwined
and inseparable in all things. Thus, the pearl symbolizes
both hope and greed, and the protagonist Kino, too, exhibits
this same duality.

2. *The Pearl:* A Parable of Hope *by Charles R. Metzger* 41

In *The Pearl* Steinbeck demonstrates the high price man can
pay for hoping. At the start of the novel, Kino is poor and
without hope that his condition will ever change. Discovery
of the pearl arouses Kino's dreams of a better life, yet his new
hope and the attendant fear of hope thwarted put Kino on a
path of almost total destruction.

3. *The Pearl:* A Novel of Disengagement
by Tetsumaro Hayashi   48

The Pearl demonstrates disengagement on two levels. First,
the pearl leads Kino to disengage from his simple yet content
life. When this leads to devastating losses, Kino must disengage himself from the lure of the pearl to find salvation.

4. Thematic Structure in *The Pearl*
by Ernest E. (Ernie) Karsten Jr.   53

The Pearl's central theme is man's existence in the context
of human relationships, which give life meaning. The
novel's structure supports this interpretation.

5. *The Pearl:* A Parable of the Human Condition
by Richard Astro   62

It is the human condition never to be satisfied with what
one has; man will risk everything to secure a better life. *The
Pearl* is Steinbeck's exploration of this condition, of man's
search for happiness.

Chapter 2: Symbols, Language, and Structural Devices

1. The Allegory of *The Pearl* by Peter Lisca 68

The Pearl is Steinbeck's allegory of the human soul. To reinforce this, Steinbeck interweaves mythical elements into the narrative, including Eden myths and mythical elements from Indian cultures.

2. Symbols and Imagery in *The Pearl* by John H. Timmerman 74

Steinbeck uses symbols and imagery to infuse *The Pearl* with meaning, including animal imagery and light and dark imagery. Too, Steinbeck creates a symbolic interplay between the Song of the Family and the Song of Evil.

3. Language Devices in *The Pearl* by John M. Nagle 84

Steinbeck's word choice, word order, and sentence structure all create and intensify meaning in his tale of the pearl.

4. The Flawed Narrative Structure of *The Pearl* by Roy Simmonds 89

The Pearl includes three distinct narrative forms: cinematic, realistic, and fabular. These all fail to some degree and—because the story line is so slight—overburden the novel.

5. Proportioning in *The Pearl* by Roland Bartel 95

A quantitative approach to *The Pearl*—analyzing the amount of space allocated to various episodes, characters, and themes—provides important clues with which to interpret the story.

Chapter 3: A Critical Selection

1. The Role of the Mountains in *The Pearl* by Louis Owens 101

The role of the mountains is often overlooked in analysis of *The Pearl*, yet the mountains are thematically and symbolically central to the novel. They not only provide evocative atmosphere, but also symbolize elemental and unconquerable forces in the story.

2. Biological Descriptions in *The Pearl* by Masanori Tokunaga 111

Steinbeck's interest in biology is clearly evident in *The Pearl*, which is infused with animalistic imagery and elaborate descriptions of living things.

3. Family Dynamic in *The Pearl* by Linda Wagner-Martin 115

The Pearl is Steinbeck's retelling of a story of a young Indian who finds a great pearl. Steinbeck adds richness and complexity to his novel by introducing key changes to the original story, namely by transforming the protagonist into a husband and father.

Chapter 4: Characters in *The Pearl*

1. *The Pearl:* Character Analysis
by Martha Heasley Cox   122

Steinbeck derived many characters in *The Pearl* from the seed story he heard in the Gulf of California. The characters, including the seemingly minor ones, provide color and meaning to the story.

2. Juana: A Woman of Worth
by Mimi Reisel Gladstein   129

Steinbeck's Juana represents a composite of the best qualities of the archetypal woman. Throughout the novel, Juana remains strong, courageous, nurturing, and wise.

3. Kino: The Ideal Man *by Sunita Jain*   134

Kino's willingness to defy a world that will not allow him to secure a better life for himself is the ultimate expression of his dignity and courage. Kino emerges from his travails as the ideal man, a group animal who retains his individuality.

4. Kino and Juana: The Transformation
by Edward E. Waldron   141

Despite the huge losses shouldered by Kino and Juana at the novel's end, there is a sense of triumph, too, in the transformation of Kino and Juana into better people.

Chronology   144

For Further Research   149

Works by John Steinbeck   152

Index   153

FOREWORD

*"'Tis the good reader that
makes the good book."*

Ralph Waldo Emerson

The story's bare facts are simple: The captain, an old and scarred seafarer, walks with a peg leg made of whale ivory. He relentlessly drives his crew to hunt the world's oceans for the great white whale that crippled him. After a long search, the ship encounters the whale and a fierce battle ensues. Finally the captain drives his harpoon into the whale, but the harpoon line catches the captain about the neck and drags him to his death.

A simple story, a straightforward plot—yet, since the 1851 publication of Herman Melville's *Moby-Dick*, readers and critics have found many meanings in the struggle between Captain Ahab and the whale. To some, the novel is a cautionary tale that depicts how Ahab's obsession with revenge leads to his insanity and death. Others believe that the whale represents the unknowable secrets of the universe and that Ahab is a tragic hero who dares to challenge fate by attempting to discover this knowledge. Perhaps Melville intended Ahab as a criticism of Americans' tendency to become involved in well-intentioned but irrational causes. Or did Melville model Ahab after himself, letting his fictional character express his anger at what he perceived as a cruel and distant god?

Although literary critics disagree over the meaning of *Moby-Dick*, readers do not need to choose one particular interpretation in order to gain an understanding of Melville's novel. Instead, by examining various analyses, they can gain numerous insights into the issues that lie under the surface of the basic plot. Studying the writings of literary critics can also aid readers in making their own assessments of *Moby-Dick* and other literary works and in developing analytical thinking skills.

The Greenhaven Literary Companion Series was created with these goals in mind. Designed for young adults, this unique anthology series provides an engaging and comprehensive introduction to literary analysis and criticism. The essays included in the Literary Companion Series are chosen for their accessibility to a young adult audience and are expertly edited in consideration of both the reading and comprehension levels of this audience. In addition, each essay is introduced by a concise summation that presents the contributing writer's main themes and insights. Every anthology in the Literary Companion Series contains a varied selection of critical essays that cover a wide time span and express diverse views. Wherever possible, primary sources are represented through excerpts from authors' notebooks, letters, and journals and through contemporary criticism.

Each title in the Literary Companion Series pays careful consideration to the historical context of the particular author or literary work. In-depth biographies and detailed chronologies reveal important aspects of authors' lives and emphasize the historical events and social milieu that influenced their writings. To facilitate further research, every anthology includes primary and secondary source bibliographies of articles and/or books selected for their suitability for young adults. These engaging features make the Greenhaven Literary Companion series ideal for introducing students to literary analysis in the classroom or as a library resource for young adults researching the world's great authors and literature.

Exceptional in its focus on young adults, the Greenhaven Literary Companion Series strives to present literary criticism in a compelling and accessible format. Every title in the series is intended to spark readers' interest in leading American and world authors, to help them broaden their understanding of literature, and to encourage them to formulate their own analyses of the literary works that they read. It is the editors' hope that young adult readers will find these anthologies to be true companions in their study of literature.

INTRODUCTION

John Steinbeck's *The Pearl* is the story of one man's search for freedom, wealth, and security. It is an outwardly simple book: the primitive Kino finds a spectacular pearl that promises a better life but ultimately rejects it after suffering loss and disillusionment. Yet as Steinbeck moves Kino on his journey, a multifaceted story emerges to the discerning reader.

The power and beauty with which Steinbeck tells his tale is widely acknowledged, but the greatness of *The Pearl* is perhaps that the narrative—despite its brevity and simplicity—is capable of supporting an array of critical approaches. First, there is the obvious sociological reading, in which Steinbeck creates a portrait of a primitive yet dignified man defeated by a predatory community that refuses to let him rise above his station in life. Other critics focus on Steinbeck's predilection toward biology and living things; *The Pearl*'s rich and highly functional animal imagery lead many to view the novel as Steinbeck's statement on ecology and the natural order of life. Still others consider the novel on a symbolic level, in which Steinbeck invests bare details with rich, underlying meaning.

These are but a few of the interpretations to which *The Pearl* lends itself. To aid the reader considering the novel's various layers of meaning, *Readings on The Pearl* includes seventeen essays that present a broad spectrum of critical opinion. Some explore a specific theme or technique. Several focus on the novel's structure or use of language. Still others consider the novel's major symbols. Several essays present analysis of *The Pearl*'s characters. The essays are arranged to make research easy and accessible. An introduction to each essay clearly summarizes the author's main ideas, highlighted by subheads in the text. A biography provides not only important information about John Steinbeck but also historical background to the novel. Other features include a chronology that places the novel in a broader historical context, an annotated table of contents, an index, and a bibliography for further research.

Readers of *The Pearl* are reminded of Steinbeck's prefatory comment to the novel: "If this story is a parable, perhaps everyone takes his own meaning from it and reads his own life into it." Taking this cue from the author, the thoughtful reader is invited to ponder this complex work. Is *The Pearl* an ecological instrument to trumpet Steinbeck's worldview? Is it a parable of the human condition? Or is it Steinbeck's social commentary on a world that beats down the underdog? Whatever meaning the reader takes, the beauty and precision of Steinbeck's prose cements *The Pearl*'s status as a classic that will continue to merit wide critical scrutiny.

JOHN STEINBECK: A BIOGRAPHY

John Steinbeck was born and raised in the Salinas Valley of west-central California. Any serious discussion of his life and work must begin here, for this fertile, beautiful California valley—extending from the Monterey Bay in the north to San Luis Obispo in the south and stretching between the ranges of the Santa Lucia and Gabilan mountains—exerted a powerful influence on the man and the writer. From this landscape of rolling hills, rugged mountains, and majestic shorelines, Steinbeck drew material for the settings, characters, and incidents of his most memorable books. Indeed, few American authors have so thoroughly mined the riches of their homeland. It is no accident, then, that so much of his fiction takes place in California, specifically in the long valley that he deeply loved, chronicled, and called home.

The California into which John Ernst Steinbeck Jr. was born on February 27, 1902, promised excitement and opportunity. Still reminiscent of its colorful frontier history and bustling gold rush days, California at the turn of the century enjoyed a healthy economy and rapid development, and an enterprising middle class was taking root. Although his parents, John Ernst Steinbeck and Olive Hamilton Steinbeck, were far from wealthy, they lived in a large, comfortable Victorian house and were socially and culturally active. The family included young John's elder sisters, ten-year-old Esther and eight-year-old Elizabeth. John's father managed a flour mill and later opened a feed-and-grain store. When the latter enterprise failed, the elder Steinbeck became an accountant.

REARING AN INTELLECTUAL

The Steinbeck home nurtured young John's budding intellect. The house was filled with books and the family read aloud to each other as entertainment. John's mother, Olive, held considerable ambitions for her only boy. Wishing to produce a cultured and educated son, she took charge of his education at an early age. To the small boy she read the classics of world literature, including the Bible when he was three, and *Robin Hood* and *Treasure Island* when he was four. Perhaps most importantly, his mother's own inquisitive nature kindled Steinbeck's imagination and capacity for wonder. As Steinbeck biographer Jackson J. Benson points out:

> It was she who planted the seed with her bedroom stories of enchanted forests, she who encouraged her son to use his imagination, to discover a world made up of both the seen and the unseen, and to perceive the nature of things intuitively and poetically, and not only by the common sense that alone was valued in the masculine society of a "frontier town."

Undoubtedly, John's mother had a great impact on John's development, but it was Steinbeck's father, not his mother, who supported his writing endeavors. In later years, Steinbeck recalled:

> In my struggle to be a writer, it was he who supported and backed me and explained me—not my mother. She wanted me desperately to be something decent like a banker. She would have liked me to be a successful writer like Tarkington but this she didn't believe I could do. But my father wanted me to be myself.... And I think he liked the complete ruthlessness of my design to be a writer in spite of mother and hell.

Steinbeck described his father as a somewhat withdrawn man, frustrated by his lack of success in business yet also strong, gentle, and sensitive. As one of Steinbeck's sisters commented about the elder Steinbeck, "He suffered for people in their trouble," perhaps accounting, in part, for Steinbeck's great humanity, his compassion for the misfits and outcasts of life.

When John was nine, he received a gift that profoundly influenced his view of language and literature:

> One day, an aunt gave me a book and fatuously ignored my resentment. I stared at the black print with hatred, and then gradually the pages opened and let me in. The magic happened. The Bible and Shakespeare and *Pilgrim's Progress* belonged to everyone. But this was mine—secretly mine. It was a cut version of the Caxton "Morte d'Arthur" of Thomas Malory. I loved the old spellings of the words—and the words no longer used. Perhaps a passionate love for the English language opened to me from this one book. I was delighted to find out paradoxes—that "cleave" means both to stick together and to cut apart.... For a long time, I had a secret language.

John read *Le Morte Darthur* with Mary, his younger sister born in 1909. Armed with their "secret language"—and fertile imaginations—the two would escape to the hills and play out the romantic adventures of King Arthur. Steinbeck's interest in Malory proved to be lifelong; years later, Arthurian themes would make their way into some of Steinbeck's most well read fiction.

John entered Salinas High School in 1915. He was somewhat of a social failure. Shy and withdrawn, he was not particularly good-looking or athletic, had no close friends, and eschewed most social activities. Academically, he was an unremarkable student, but he excelled in English and eventually became editor of the school yearbook, in which his first published work appeared. These early forays in yearbook writing clearly show young Steinbeck's emerging wit: "The English room, which is just down the hall from the office, is the sanctuary of Shakespeare, the temple of Milton and Byron, and the terror of Freshmen. English is a kind of high brow idea of the American language. A hard job is made of nothing at all and nothing at all is made of a hard job. It is in this room and this room alone that the English language is spoken." By the end of his freshman year, Steinbeck had set his sights on becoming a writer.

THE RELUCTANT SCHOLAR

Steinbeck's success in high school English and his ambition to write prompted him to begin his studies at Stanford University as an English major in the fall of 1919. His college career proved intermittent and erratic; he attended classes off and on for six years and never earned a degree. While his performance at the university was for the most part mediocre, several important events in this period left their mark on Steinbeck. First, he took a writing course under the talented but demanding Edith Ronald Mirrielees. The strict professor liked Steinbeck's writing—she thought his work should be published—but challenged him to pare excess words and ornamentation. At first, Steinbeck did not take this criticism well: He loved words and wanted to exercise his vocabulary through his writing. Eventually, however, Mirrielees won him over and he worked to develop a more disciplined prose style. About her demand for conciseness, Steinbeck said in a letter to a friend, "She does one thing for you. She makes you get over what you want to say." Under her tutelage, Steinbeck honed his writing skills, creating the lean, terse narrative style that would later earn him praise.

Also of major significance was workingman experience gained during Steinbeck's frequent hiatuses from Stanford.

Steinbeck spent his time away from school working for wages on road gangs and commercial farms, notably on the sprawling Spreckels Sugar Ranch, which was actually a number of ranches dotting the land from King City in the south to Santa Clara in the north. Spreckels grew sugar beets primarily, but also raised alfalfa and hay as well as some cattle. Its huge beet crop was planted and harvested by hired hands—bindle stiffs, or hobos, and migrants—who traveled to whichever Spreckels ranch had work and stayed as long as their labor was needed.

To understand the impact this job had on Steinbeck, it is important to note that Steinbeck came of age during a time when California's booming agricultural industry was plagued by labor problems. Commercial growers relied on cheap, seasonal labor, often taking advantage of the flood of migrant workers who roamed the west, looking for work. Many were of Mexican, Japanese, or Filipino descent. Their lives were marked by poverty and few enjoyed more than the most meager living conditions. Although the farm industry was undergoing a historic transformation—the advent of high-tech farm equipment rendered many workers obsolete—for a time in the 1920s Steinbeck became part of this working culture.

Steinbeck's time at Spreckels brought the impressionable young writer into direct contact with a kaleidoscope of characters, most from the lower echelon of society. Steinbeck got on well with his fellow workers despite their lower-class status. He regarded them with warmth and compassion and without condescension or mere pity. He was deeply moved by their struggles. Most importantly, he discovered that their basic human qualities—their needs and desires—were not so very different from the rest of mankind's, despite differences in race, origins, or social position. Steinbeck's compassion for these people would manifest itself years later in many of his most memorable novels.

PURSUING A WRITING CAREER

Not caring to fulfill the academic requirements for a degree, Steinbeck left Stanford for good in 1925. In June of that year he packed his bags and headed for Lake Tahoe, where he had been offered a job as a maintenance man. Unsure of his future but certain that he wanted to make his way as a writer, his goal was to earn enough money to travel to New York City. There, he believed, he could launch his writing career. By November he took a job on a freighter bound for New York. The sea voyage through the tropical waters of the Caribbean and the Panama Canal piqued Steinbeck's writer's instinct. Fascinated by the vivid scenery, Steinbeck would fictionalize his impressions in his first book, *Cup of Gold.*

After the exhilarating sea voyage, Steinbeck's arrival in New York was somewhat of a shock. He recalled in an article years later: "It horrified me. There was something monstrous about it—the tall buildings looming to the sky and the lights shining through the falling snow. I crept ashore—frightened and cold and with a touch of panic in my stomach." Yet Steinbeck was determined to see his work published, and he set to the task with alacrity and gusto. Writing stories on the side, he earned a living as a construction worker and later as a reporter at the *New York American,* where he found he did not enjoy news writing; its rigid parameters did not allow the creative expression that Steinbeck craved.

This was a grim time for Steinbeck. Not one of his stories was published, and he was terminated from his job at the newspaper. The only bright spot in Steinbeck's New York stay was one publisher's enthusiasm for one of Steinbeck's stories. Unfortunately, the story was never published. Bitterly disappointed and at the end of his rope, Steinbeck packed his rejected manuscripts and boarded a freighter headed for San Francisco.

REFUGE IN WRITING

Back in California, Steinbeck secured a job as the caretaker of a huge estate at Lake Tahoe, which he would call home for the next two years. Considering that Steinbeck often grappled with self-doubt and a fear of loneliness, his choice was curious: As the first snowstorm of the season descended upon Steinbeck's tiny cabin, he faced loneliness and isolation more powerful than any he had previously experienced. But paradoxically, the solitude of the Sierra Nevada—he was snowed in for eight months—lent itself well to Steinbeck's singular pursuit; with very few demands on his time, he finished many short stories and, by February 1928, the novel *Cup of Gold.* He sent the manuscript to former Stanford classmate Ted Miller in New York. Miller had promised to place Steinbeck's manuscripts with publishers, and in January 1929, Steinbeck received the happy news that McBride and Company would publish *Cup of Gold.* The reviews were tepid and the book was not widely read; nevertheless, its publication marked the onset of a happy and prolific decade in which

Steinbeck would shine, both personally and professionally.

In Lake Tahoe, Steinbeck had fallen in love with a vacationing secretary named Carol Henning. The couple married in January 1930 and settled in Los Angeles. Carol recognized Steinbeck's talent and encouraged his writing endeavors. Marriage seemed to agree with Steinbeck, and the contented writer pursued his literary career with vigor. He wrote, and Carol typed and edited. About her invaluable assistance, Steinbeck wrote in a letter to a friend, "It's a dirty shame Carol has to work so hard. She's putting in nine hours a day at it. I wish I could do it but my typing is so very lousy." In another letter he proclaimed, "Carol is a good influence on my work. . . . I have the time and the energy and it gives me pleasure to work, and now I do not seem to have to fight as much reluctance to work as I used to have."

About this time, Steinbeck met marine biologist Ed Ricketts, who would prove to be the greatest single influence on Steinbeck's artistic development. To Steinbeck, Ricketts was a fascinating character. He was exceedingly well read in many areas. He had a reputation not only for his sharp, analytical mind, but also for his wry sense of humor. Like Steinbeck, Ricketts loved to talk, analyze, and philosophize. He could debate a wide range of topics, and he enjoyed playing devil's advocate. In short, he was the perfect companion for Steinbeck. The importance of their subsequent eighteen-year friendship cannot be understated. Ricketts was Steinbeck's closest friend, mentor, and partner. His biological views suffuse much of Steinbeck's work. He even served as the model for some of Steinbeck's most memorable characters, including Doc in *Cannery Row.*

Satisfying personal relationships aside, Steinbeck was in the same trouble financially as the rest of the country. The stock market had crashed in 1929, a disaster that heralded severe economic hardship across the globe. Millions of workers were unemployed and businesses and banks were failing across the nation. Yet the Steinbecks were somewhat insulated from the effects of the Great Depression for several reasons, as Steinbeck recalled years later in an *Esquire* article:

> The Depression was no financial shock to me. I didn't have any money to lose, but in common with millions I did dislike hunger and cold. I had two assets. My father owned a tiny three-room cottage in Pacific Grove in California, and he let me live in it without rent. That was the first safety. Pacific Grove is on the sea. That was the second. People in inland cities or in the closed and shuttered industrial cemeteries had

greater problems than I. Given the sea a man must be very stupid to starve. The great reservoir of food is always available. I took a large part of my protein food from the sea.

I must drop the "I" for "we" now, for there was a fairly large group of us poor kids, all living alike. We pooled our troubles, our money when we had some, our inventiveness, and our pleasures. I remember it as a warm and friendly time. Only illness frightened us.

About the time he met Ricketts, Steinbeck was recommended to the literary agency of Mavis McIntosh and Elizabeth Otis, who took him on as a client in 1931. Their professional association would last throughout Steinbeck's career. When they met, Steinbeck was plodding through some frustrating projects: *Dissonant Harmony*, a novel that he never completed and about which not much is known, and *Murder at Full Moon*, a detective story that was never published. He was working intermittently on *To an Unknown God* and *Pastures of Heaven*, ten collected short stories about a family named Munroe. *Pastures of Heaven* was published in 1932; an encouraged Steinbeck returned to rewriting *To an Unknown God*, a historical saga of the Salinas Valley to which Steinbeck was so emotionally tied. At Ricketts's prompting, he changed the title to *To a God Unknown*. Meanwhile, *Pastures of Heaven* garnered bad reviews and sold so poorly that the book had to be remaindered before the publishers went bankrupt.

A CHANGE IN FORTUNE

"This has been a very bad year all around for us," Steinbeck wrote in a letter to college friend Carl Wilhelmson. Then, Steinbeck's mother suffered a stroke, rendering her a helpless invalid. John and Carol spent a great deal of time caring for both Olive and the grief-stricken elder Steinbeck. Despite financial hardship and family tragedy, however, several fortuitous events occurred during this time. In conversations with his father, Steinbeck conceived the idea for the collection of stories that would become *The Red Pony*, one of Steinbeck's most loved creations, featuring a boy who is given a colt. He also became interested in a work about poor Mexicans called *paisanos*. Their story, *Tortilla Flat*, would skyrocket Steinbeck to fame.

In the meantime, Steinbeck was refining *To a God Unknown*. The book was published in 1933. The same year, the *North American Review* published two of the pony stories. In 1934 the *North American Review* published the short story

"The Murder," for which Steinbeck won the O. Henry Award for the best story of the year. At last, Steinbeck was enjoying literary acceptance, and his happiness was overshadowed only by his mother's death in 1934.

NATIONAL RECOGNITION

Ironically, Steinbeck was having a rough time getting *Tortilla Flat* published. The novel that would eventually land on the best-seller list was rejected by five publishers. Steinbeck's fortune changed, however, in January 1935, when he was contacted by New York publisher Pascal Covici, who had read and liked *Pastures of Heaven*. Covici offered to not only publish *Tortilla Flat* but also reissue Steinbeck's earlier books. *Tortilla Flat* hit the bookstands in May 1935. It was an immediate success. The bittersweet story follows a group of free-spirited *paisanos* who had been likened to Arthurian knights. Readers not only appreciated the droll humor but also were deeply moved by the pathos of the comic characters. Sadly, Steinbeck's father did not live to see the public's reaction to *Tortilla Flat;* the elder Steinbeck died a few days before the book was released.

With *Tortilla Flat* Steinbeck finally received recognition as a literary artist. Although Steinbeck disliked being a public figure, he was happy with the book's success and enthused about his next project, a story of two Marxists who attempt to organize an agricultural strike. The book's subject matter paralleled the labor movement sweeping the nation's agricultural regions—and the attempts to repress it. Steinbeck's book, titled *In Dubious Battle*, was released in 1936 and sold moderately well.

OF MICE AND MEN

Throughout his life, Steinbeck suffered misgivings about his literary ability and shunned being a public figure. Fighting the demands of celebrity, Steinbeck and his wife bought a piece of land on the outskirts of Los Gatos, a quiet community just north of Monterey. As Carol oversaw the building of a house, John began working on a new novel, tentatively titled *Something That Happened*. The story traced life among the hired hands of a Salinas Valley ranch. Undoubtedly, the story was strongly influenced by Steinbeck's college-age experiences as a laborer on the Spreckels Sugar Ranch.

Steinbeck finished a manuscript quickly, but at the end of May he had a "minor tragedy," which he humorously recounted to Elizabeth Otis:

Minor tragedy stalked. My setter pup left alone one night, made confetti of about half of my ms. book. Two months work to do over again. It sets me back. There was no other draft. I was pretty mad but the poor little fellow may have been acting critically. I didn't want to ruin a good dog for a ms. I'm not sure is good at all. He only got an ordinary spanking with his punishment flyswatter. But there's the work to do over from the start.

He continued working on the novel, but under a new title suggested by Ed Ricketts, *Of Mice and Men.* Steinbeck finished his short novel—it was only a little more than thirty thousand words—in the summer of 1936. His agents and editor praised the manuscript and accepted it immediately. Published in 1937, *Of Mice and Men* was an instant best-seller.

An important event occurred while Steinbeck was finishing revisions of *Of Mice and Men:* He served a stint as a reporter for the *San Francisco News.* The newspaper asked him to report on the conditions of the migrant laborers who flooded California at harvest time. This task required Steinbeck to visit the migrant camps and record his impressions. To maintain anonymity, Steinbeck wore old, worn clothing. Behind the wheel of a ramshackle bakery truck, Steinbeck observed firsthand the adversity—starvation, violence, disease—the migrants were forced to endure. His chronicles of their sad plight were published in October 1936 as a series of articles titled "The Harvest Gypsies." His moving narrative of families such as this generated great public sympathy:

Four nights ago the mother had a baby in the tent, on the dirty carpet. It was born dead, which was just as well because she could not have fed it at the breast; her own diet will not produce milk.

After it was born and she had seen that it was dead, the mother rolled over and lay still for two days. She is up today, tottering around. The last baby, born less than a year ago, lived a week. This woman's eyes have the glazed, faraway look of a sleepwalker's eyes.

She does not wash clothes any more. The drive that makes for cleanliness has been drained out of her and she hasn't the energy. The husband was a share-cropper once, but he couldn't make it go. Now he has lost even his desire to talk. . . .

The children do not even go to the willow clump any more. They squat where they are and kick a little dirt. The father is vaguely aware that there is a culture of hookworm in the mud along the river bank. He knows the children will get it on their bare feet.

But he hasn't the will nor the energy to resist. Too many things have happened to him.

This experience not only stirred Steinbeck's sense of social injustice, but was also a prelude to *The Grapes of Wrath*, Steinbeck's magnum opus.

THE PUBLIC SPOTLIGHT

In California, the Steinbecks purchased a home on fifty acres of land. Encouraged by the success of his recent books, Steinbeck took advantage of the quiet refuge to begin his "big book" about migrant laborers. Since his assignment for the *San Francisco News*, Steinbeck had been searching for a vehicle that would bring their plight to prominence. The result was *The Grapes of Wrath*, focusing on the dispossessed dust bowl farmers and their grim pilgrimage to California farm country. The book was published in April 1939. Despite Steinbeck's doubts that the book would be popular, its release was followed by astonishing international acclaim. It quickly rose to the top of the best-seller list. Along with its sensational popularity came a flood of outrage, particularly from the agricultural industry. The ensuing controversy only served to keep the book in the news, drawing even more readers. By the end of the year, more than 430,000 copies had been sold, a figure second only to *Gone with the Wind*. With *The Grapes of Wrath*, Steinbeck had irrevocably cemented his position in the public spotlight.

The demands of public life began to take their toll on Steinbeck and his marriage. Always one to shun publicity, Steinbeck often left Carol to deal with a constant onslaught of letters and visitors and celebrity obligations. Under the strain, their arguments increased in frequency. During a trip to Hollywood to visit the filming of a Steinbeck novel, the two split up. During this time, Steinbeck met and fell in love with Gwendolyn Conger, an aspiring actress-singer. Not totally committed to ending his faltering marriage, however, he managed a reconciliation with Carol, even as tensions between the two remained high.

While trying to mend his marriage during the summer of 1939, Steinbeck spent a great deal of time with Ed Ricketts. Steinbeck wanted to learn as much about marine biology as he could. The two friends spent hours combing the tidepools of California, collecting biological specimens and discussing marine animals and ecology. Ricketts believed that the ecology of the seashore could lend insight into man's place in the world. As Ricketts observed: "Who would see a replica of man's social structure has only to examine the abundant and various life of the tidepools, where miniature communal societies wage dubious battle against equally potent societies in which the individual is paramount, with trends shifting, maturing, or dying out, with all the living organisms balanced against the limitations of the dead kingdom of rocks and currents and temperatures and dissolved gases." Under Rickett's influence, Steinbeck became increasingly committed to an ecological view of the world, an idea that would take shape in *The Pearl.*

With their common passion, Ricketts and Steinbeck conceived a trip to Mexico so that they could survey the rich ecosystem of the Gulf of California, called the Sea of Cortez in Mexico. Steinbeck hoped to establish a reputation with the scientific community by publishing the results of such an expedition. Scientific aspirations aside, however, the prospect of a romantic seafaring quest surely piqued Steinbeck's sense of adventure. To accommodate their research, the two avid researchers chartered a fishing boat, the *Western Flyer*, which they filled with laboratory equipment and other supplies. On March 11, 1940, Steinbeck, Carol, Ricketts, and a small crew left Monterey and set sail for the Gulf of California.

Throughout the trip, Steinbeck and Ricketts took great care collecting specimens and recording observations. Steinbeck, in a collaborative effort with Ricketts, documented the results of their studies in *The Sea of Cortez: A Leisurely Journal of Travel and Research*, a nonfiction account of their expedition. Years later, in 1951, Steinbeck would publish *The Log from the Sea of Cortez*, which also records many events of this trip.

Steinbeck enjoyed a wealth of new experiences in the Gulf of California, and he was particularly fascinated with the native pearl fishermen of Mexico. In a section of *The Log from the Sea of Cortez*, dated March 20, 1940, Steinbeck recounts a story he heard when the *Western Flyer* docked at La Paz:

An event which happened at La Paz in recent years is typical of such places. An Indian boy by accident found a pearl of great size, an unbelievable pearl. He knew its value was so great that he need never work again. In his one pearl he had the ability to be drunk as long as he wished, to marry any one of a number of girls, and to make many more a little happy too. In his great pearl lay salvation, for he could in advance purchase masses sufficient to pop him out of Purgatory like a squeezed watermelon seed. In addition he could shift a number of dead relatives a little nearer to Paradise. He went to La Paz with his pearl in his hand and his future clear into eternity in his heart. He took his pearl to a broker and was offered so little he grew angry, for he knew he was cheated. Then he carried his pearl to another broker and was offered the same amount. After a few more visits he came to know that the brokers were only the many hands of one head and that he could not sell his pearl for more. He took it to the beach and hid it under a stone, and that night he was clubbed into unconsciousness and his clothing was searched. The next night he slept at the house of a friend and his friend and he were injured and bound and the whole house searched. Then he went inland to lose his pursuers and he was waylaid and tortured. But he was very angry now and he knew what he must do. Hurt as he was he crept back to La Paz in the night and he skulked like a hunted fox to the beach and took out his pearl from under the stone. Then he cursed it and threw it as far as he could into the channel. He was a free man again with his soul in danger and his food and shelter insecure. And he laughed a great deal about it.

This story undoubtedly planted the seed that would become *The Pearl*. Four years would elapse, however, before Steinbeck would write his version of the pearl story.

A BUSY DECADE

In 1940, Steinbeck won the Pulitzer Prize for *The Grapes of Wrath*, marking the onset of a prolific decade. He spent the forties in a whirlwind of writing, researching, and traveling, including many moves between New York and California. In Mexico City, he observed the filming of his book *The Forgotten Village*, which focuses on life in a small Mexican village. He spent time in Hollywood for the filming of *Tortilla Flat*. As World War II captured the attention of the world, the U.S. government recruited Steinbeck to produce propaganda tales. He wrote *The Moon Is Down*, a grim chronicle of a small European town occupied by Nazis. He also churned out *Bombs Away: The Story of a Bomber Team* and the script for the film *Lifeboat*, a war-morale movie.

Steinbeck's marriage to Carol had deteriorated irrevocably. The couple were divorced in 1943. Soon after, in March 1943, Steinbeck married Gwen Conger. In June, Steinbeck left his new bride for a job in England as a war correspondent for the *Herald-Tribune*. Shortly after, he transferred to North Africa to report on military activities there. He often disregarded his own personal safety and entered combat zones so that he could closely observe events as they unfolded. He even reported activity in the midst of battle. His vivid war accounts not only stirred thousands of readers but also left a deep impression on Steinbeck himself.

Returning from his wartime duty, Steinbeck turned his attention to a host of writing projects. In an attempt to take his mind off of the war, he wrote *Cannery Row* in just six weeks. His first son, Thom, was born just after he completed the manuscript in August 1944. *Cannery Row*, the humorous story of a Monterey waterfront community, was published the following January. Following *Cannery Row*'s well-received release, an invigorated Steinbeck set to finish a novelette which was already well under way. Tentatively titled, "The Pearl of La Paz," it first appeared in a December 1945 issue of *Woman's Home Companion* under the title "The Pearl of the World." The book form, titled simply *The Pearl*, was published in December 1947; a motion picture based on the novel was released simultaneously.

In his retelling of the pearl story, Steinbeck drew upon his experiences in the Gulf of California; much of the material is readily apparent in *The Log from the Sea of Cortez*. Most obviously, *The Pearl* is Steinbeck's retelling of the story he heard at La Paz, as documented in *The Log*. Interestingly, however, while Steinbeck thought the seed story seemed true, he noted that "it is so much like a parable that it almost can't be," a story that is "far too reasonable to be true." So, while he kept the basic story intact, Steinbeck introduced several changes, perhaps to make his tale more "believable." Most notably, he transformed the young Indian boy to a man named Kino who has a wife and young son. With this key change, Steinbeck elevated the simple Mexican story to one that reaches tragic proportions; Kino acknowledges that the pearl is the conveyor of greed and evil only after it brings about the death of his son.

Too, many of Steinbeck's descriptions in *The Pearl* correspond closely with recorded observations from his time in the Gulf of California; Kino's dress, equipment, and livelihood, and much of the scenery, including the landscapes of the mountains and seas, are readily apparent in *The Log*. Steinbeck's biological view, honed during his Mexico adventure, is clearly evident in passages of *The Pearl*, such as this description which opens chapter two: "The town lay on a broad estuary, its old yellow plastered buildings hugging the beach. And on the beach the white and blue canoes that came from Nayarit were drawn up. . . . The beach was yellow sand, but at the water's edge a rubble of shell and algae took its place. Fiddler crabs bubbled and sputtered in their holes in the sand, and in the shallows little lobsters popped in and out of their tiny homes in the rubble and sand."

Such eloquent descriptions, coupled with the story's compelling messages about the nature of good and evil and man's

covetous nature, ensured *The Pearl*'s success in the book-
stores, although the novel received disparate critical reviews.
The Wayward Bus, an amusing story about a busload of colorful characters, was also written during this period. It too
sold well.

PERSONAL STRIFE

The Steinbecks' second son, John, was born in August 1946.
While Steinbeck loved his children, his marriage was not a
happy one. Conditions went from bad to worse when Steinbeck received the devastating news in 1948 that Ed Ricketts
had been killed in a car accident. A grief-stricken Steinbeck
wrote in a letter to his friend Bo Beskow, "There died the
greatest man I have known and the best teacher. It is going to
take a long time to reorganize my thinking and my planning
without him." Ricketts's death marked the beginning of a
dark time in Steinbeck's life. After Ricketts's funeral, Gwen
asked Steinbeck for a divorce. Steinbeck was deeply sor-
rowed by a second failed marriage and financially stressed
by the terms of the divorce settlement. Steinbeck's books
were selling well, but not well enough to meet alimony and
child support obligations. Steinbeck returned to his family
home in Pacific Grove to heal his wounds, seeking solace, as
usual, in his writing.

Although the early years of the fifties were difficult, Steinbeck's spirit was returning. His personal life improved when
he married Elaine Scott, ex-wife of the actor Zachary Scott, in
1950. This marriage was happy and harmonious, and Steinbeck set about his writing with renewed vigor. He completed
a screenplay for *Viva Zapata!*, about the exploits of Mexican
revolutionary Emiliano Zapata, and published *Burning
Bright*, a short novel in play form that was produced as a
Broadway play. In February 1951, Steinbeck began work on
East of Eden, the saga of two families set in the Salinas Valley. It was published in 1952 and quickly became a best-
seller despite harsh critics. Next, he revised *Cannery Row* under the title *Sweet Thursday*, which was published in 1954.
Again, reviews were unfavorable. In 1956, Steinbeck began a
book based on the retelling of Sir Thomas Malory's *Le Morte
Darthur*, the story he had loved as a child. This would be
published posthumously as *The Acts of King Arthur and His
Noble Knights*. In 1957, *The Short Reign of Pippin IV* was published. It sold extremely well, but like Steinbeck's other recent work, received poor reviews.

Steinbeck was frustrated by the poor critical response to his recent novels. Then, in 1959 he suffered what appeared to be a stroke, forcing him to take time off from his writing to rest. His self-confidence continued to wane. Nevertheless, in a writing frenzy, he took up his pen and wrote *The Winter of Our Discontent.* Even before its publication in June 1961, he set off on a journey across America in a camper with Elaine's poodle Charley. This pilgrimage became the subject of *Travels with Charley in Search of America.* A few months after its publication in 1962, Steinbeck learned that he had been awarded the Nobel Prize for literature.

Steinbeck spent his last years involved in political affairs. In January 1961, he was an invited guest at John F. Kennedy's inauguration. After the president's assassination in 1963, Steinbeck became friends with Kennedy's successor, Lyndon B. Johnson. In the midsixties he reported on the war on Vietnam for *Newsday,* a Long Island daily. Seized by severe back pain on his return from traveling, he never fully recovered and suffered for his last year and a half. Steinbeck died in New York on December 20, 1968, at the age of sixty-six. Shortly before his death, he told Elaine, "No man should be buried in alien soil," to which she replied, "I know what you are telling me. You won't be." True to her word, Elaine returned Steinbeck's ashes to his native ground in Salinas, California, where they rest today.

CHAPTER 1

Important Themes in *The Pearl*

The Nature of Good and Evil in *The Pearl*

Michael J. Meyer

In *The Pearl*, Steinbeck offers a moral lesson about the nature of good and evil, writes Michael J. Meyer. Steinbeck rejects a black-and-white code of absolute good and evil, Meyer argues; rather, Steinbeck illustrates that good and evil are inseparably intertwined, and that this duality is essential to existence. Thus, the ambiguous nature of the pearl—which at first symbolizes beauty and hope but becomes gray and ulcerous—parallels Kino's duality, as he himself becomes cold and hardened. Clinging to absolutes— the goodness of the pearl, for example—results in Kino's downfall; accepting moral ambiguity brings him salvation. Meyer is an assistant professor of English at Concordia College in Wisconsin.

Many critics have persisted in criticizing Steinbeck's didacticism and seeing only the black-and-white absolutes they expect in parables rather than the complex moral lesson that the author provides through his setting, characters, and symbols. In this lesson Steinbeck asserts that duality undergirds all of man's actions, and that intertwining good and evil are a part of each postlapsarian [time after the fall of man] human.

Nevertheless, mankind generally wishes to deny such a frustrating state of being and pretend that it doesn't exist. Steinbeck illustrates this well in Kino and Juana, his protagonists, who reluctantly experience duality. These primitive natives undergo an initiation rite in the novel similar to what Adam and Eve experienced when they ate from the tree of knowledge of good and evil. This initiation destroys the couple's naïve concept of what man and the world are like and leaves them bereft but wiser in their knowledge of

Excerpted from Michael J. Meyer, "Precious Bane: Mining the Fool's Gold of *The Pearl*," in Jackson J. Benson, ed., *The Short Novels of John Steinbeck.* Copyright 1990, Duke University Press. Reprinted with permission.

themselves and of their society. Their discovery dispels the illusions of the "good" that surrounds them but also frustrates them as they struggle to cope with a reality which almost always involves a paradoxical yoking of opposites.

The yoking of opposites is most obvious in Steinbeck's use of imagery in the novel to portray an intersecting dichotomy of good versus evil. In the novel, sights and sounds as well as symbols are used to compose a pattern of images that offer evidence of the morally ambiguous state that Kino and Juana must contend with.

LIGHT VERSUS DARKNESS

The first major image Steinbeck uses is a traditional one: light versus darkness. Although several critics have noted that *The Pearl* begins with sunrise and ends in sunset, few have noted that neither the symbolic light nor the lack of it remains the dominant visual image. Instead, light and darkness mingle together to form gray areas where good and evil are inextricably mixed.

Consequently, the reader cannot surmise that the purity and goodness which begin the novel are destroyed and blackened by the sunset which ends the work. In fact, the light/dark imagery fluctuates between positive and negative connotations just as good and evil do. In addition, the sunrise which begins the day is accompanied by another "positive" image—the harmony of music, the Song of the Family. This sound image also persists in the novel, using another traditional presentation of good's conflict with evil: harmony versus disharmony. Through this image Steinbeck affirms that the beautiful music and its lyric melody, like the early morning, cannot be maintained without the eventual intrusion of discord and dark. As Steinbeck stated in a letter to his close friend Pascal Covici in January 1941: "It seems that two forces are necessary in man before he is a man. [He is] a product of all his filth and disease and meanness, his hunger and cruelty. Cure those and you would have not man but an entirely new species you wouldn't recognize and probably wouldn't like."

Here Steinbeck seems to agree with philosopher David Bakan, who postulates that duality is essential to mankind when he states that "the most critical paradox that man must live with, is the possibility that all that is characteristically associated with evil is, in some way, intimately intertwined with good, the notion that the sins of mankind, sex, aggression and avarice, are related to the survival of mankind." It is thus not surprising that Steinbeck's use of images becomes syncretic [fusing different forms], merging together the various sides of objects and symbols and presenting both the positive and the negative simultaneously. For example, Steinbeck notes that the Song of the Family is quite flexible, and, even though it only has three notes, it possesses an endless variety of intervals. Similarly, although the melody signifies safety, warmth, and wholeness for the couple, it is significant that sometimes the song rises to a sobbing or aching chord that catches in the throat. Ultimately the dual image will expand until the clash of different melodies will indicate Kino's despair at ever being able to achieve harmony in his world.

The merged images of dissonance and darkness continue to preempt the bright music of Juana and are depicted as a threatening song which emanates from a scorpion, Steinbeck's first symbol of the sin and evil which threaten every man. This scorpion and its song conspire against even the innocent tiny baby Coyotito. However, the fact that this scorpion is portrayed as a random evil which invades the couple's lives seems to indicate Steinbeck's belief that the dark side of man's soul is uncontrollable and will eventually attack even the most peaceful, innocent, and harmonious of lives. In short, once again the novel asserts that if a mixture of good and evil is essential to existence, attempts to see only one side of the human condition are futile.

FAILURE TO ACKNOWLEDGE EVIL

However, Juana and Kino, as representatives of an innocent Adam and Eve in the garden, are unaccustomed to the darkness and disharmony that infiltrate human society. Up to this point their lives have been so sheltered that they mistakenly believe that evil exists only in obvious outside forces like the scorpion. Such a force can be smashed into paste by the human hand or foot, and definitely will be overcome in a matter of time. However, once the sting of the evil one touches the baby, his parents begin to discover that their analysis is mistaken and that the evil that the scorpion embodies is impossible to wipe out. Thus, although the physical scorpion is destroyed, it is evident that another springs up in the city of La Paz. Despite the promises of peace that its name suggests, the city provides still further duality as Steinbeck examines the "civilized" community and compares its evil with the scorpion while contrasting it with the goodness of Juana and Kino's primitive existence. As soon as the native couple enter the city seeking help, they begin to learn the lesson that the town does not contain the same warmth and wholeness of their small thatched hut. Moreover, they also note the absence of the moral absolutes that simplified their lives. In the city the evil darkness intermingles intangibly with the good light. It cannot be extracted by folk cures, religion, or ancient spells because it runs rampant among the so-called civilized people, whose avarice and jealousy destroy their potential for good.

For example, the doctor who is so essential to the cure of Coyotito is initially associated with the light of education and the blessing of good health. He is seen by the couple as a potential savior, but actually he is the epitome of evil. The ability to distinguish good from evil is thus seen as difficult, at best, and Steinbeck reinforces this dilemma by describing the fine line that separates the two opposites as a "hazy mirage." As Steinbeck describes nature in chapter 2 as poison fish hiding in eel grass and dogs and pigs who feed off the dead, even the positive qualities of the pure surroundings of Juana and Kino are seen as questionable and hiding unknowns. This, of course, parallels a similar uncertainty for Kino and Juana about what is good and what is evil.

MORAL AMBIGUITY

Soon the couple will find that nothing is sure and solid, and that moral ambiguity is man's heritage. Yet most critics of *The Pearl* have persisted in looking for absolutes and defining the meaning of images within strict boundaries which ultimately did not hold up under close scrutiny. But Steinbeck's parable is not so easily resolved. Chapter 3 begins in brightness as good returns in the form of the great pearl which Kino discovers, the Pearl of the World, gigantic in size and shape. Although not all readers are aware of his literary allusion to the medieval poem also entitled "The Pearl," Steinbeck carefully suggests that even though the gem appears to offer salvation, it is yet another example of the intermixture of good and evil. Specifically, the initial description points out the irony of the pearl's development. It was created because an irritant, a grain of sand, penetrated the oyster's shell and lodged within it. In this incident Steinbeck shows how negatives are at times strangely transformed into positives, and worthless grains of sand become priceless treasures as the oyster works to dispel or neutralize the invading grain, which may cause life-threatening problems.

Once again, Steinbeck reintroduces and merges his imagery as the symbolic pearl, which is precious and beyond price, is associated with light. For example, it is "as perfect as the moon. It captured the light and gave it back in silver incandescence. It was as large as a sea-gull's egg. It was the greatest pearl in the world." Yet at the same time the author also uses his light image negatively to stress the moral ambiguity of the gem by stating that the treasure has a ghostly gleam and that Kino mistrusts his perceptions and wonders if the prize might be more illusion than reality.

Elsewhere Steinbeck returns to the music imagery, the Song of the Family, and joins it with the Song of the Pearl That Might Be. At this point the pearl tune is described as a countermelody that blends in with the dominant music, but later in the novel the Song of the Pearl will be associated with something infinitely evil as the narrator notes that "the essence of the pearl was mixed with the essence of men and a curious dark residue was precipitated . . . the schemes, the plans, . . . the lusts, the hungers and . . . he [Kino] became curiously every man's enemy."

Yet Juana and Kino are reluctant to acknowledge the duality they are confronting, for it seems as if their long-sought-for salvation has arrived. Warm and happy in their newfound success and good luck, they can only believe that the music of the family has merged with the music of the pearl so that each beautifies the other.

Kino's Aspirations

Influenced by this belief, Kino begins to dream of new values and goals, of the light, harmony, and good that the pearl can bring to his life. By seeing only the benefits that the pearl of great price can bring to him, he ignores the treasure's potential for evil, and, unfortunately, his "positive" desires for material goods and for health and education for his son create a negative force in his life. As pride and conceit over his ownership begin to dominate his life, he turns from his former kindly disposition into a man as ruthless and evil as any of the townspeople. A similar irony exists in the fact

HUMAN DUALITY

In The Log from the Sea of Cortez, *Steinbeck discusses how humans are marked by universally recognized good and bad qualities that result in an interesting ethical paradox.*

There is a strange duality in the human which makes for an ethical paradox. We have definitions of good qualities and of bad; not changing things, but generally considered good and bad throughout the ages and throughout the species. Of the good, we think always of wisdom, tolerance, kindliness, generosity, humility; and the qualities of cruelty, greed, self-interest, graspingness, and rapacity are universally considered undesirable. And yet in our structure of society, the so-called and considered good qualities are invariably concomitants of failure, while the bad ones are the cornerstones of success. A man—a viewing-point man—while he will love the abstract good qualities and detest the abstract bad, will nevertheless envy and admire the person who through possessing the bad qualities has succeeded economically and socially, and will hold in contempt that person whose good qualities have caused failure.

John Steinbeck, *The Log from the Sea of Cortez,* 1941.

that although the pearl may solve Kino's problems, Steinbeck reiterates after its discovery that "the dark is almost in." Eventually the coming night becomes a threatening dark that will reveal the greed of Kino's neighbors as they try to steal the pearl from him, turning his dreams into nightmares.

The symbolic pearl is combined with the sight and sound images here as the music of evil suddenly returns to Kino's ears, signifying the duality of the townspeople and the church but also the duality of the gem itself. This music image is described as shrill, as opposed to the sweet music Kino formerly heard from the pearl. Kino, once so positive about his find, now wonders whether anyone or anything can be trusted; his simple naïvete is being systematically destroyed. Even the medicine prescribed by the doctor is questionable, as Kino cannot help but wonder whether the prescription itself is not evil masquerading as good and whether Coyotito's illness has been caused by the doctor in order to gain the pearl for himself. Such duplicity continues in the narration when the doctor arrives and denies having heard of Kino's good fortune, thus craftily causing Kino to betray the secret hiding place of the treasure.

INEXTRICABLE SYMBOLS

The symbols of the scorpion and the pearl, once quite separate and opposite, are now strangely joined, and just as the neighbors were previously associated with the characteristics of the scorpion, so Kino is associated with the pearl. He is no longer pure, but like the oyster is infected by the sands of mistrust and fear. Steinbeck describes the hardness growing over him, but what results for Kino is no treasure. This hardness suggests not wealth but man's animal-like state, where faith and hope in goodness and light and harmony have disappeared as human traits. Soon Kino dreams of darkness, not only a darkness which blots out his own dreams for success but one that also denies the potential of Coyotito's future. Combining this depressing action with sound, Kino begins to recognize that every sound in the world is now an indicator of a dark thing. Kino is transformed into a raging beast, and suddenly the evil side of a primitive life-style is exposed. The formerly docile Kino, his very life now threatened, transforms into a wild animal whose one law is the dark violence of the jungle. Kino has grown in hatred, sin, and wrongdoing, and Steinbeck again suggests that he is similar to the evil part of the pearl: hard, cold, and unyielding.

Despite the use of the negative parallel, Kino still does not understand the concept of the duality of all things. The pearl is still seen as positive because it will provide for a good, the healing of the baby. Yet shortly thereafter, Steinbeck removes this motive as the poison appears to recede from Coyotito's body and it is no longer necessary to use the pearl to obtain the needed payment for the doctor's services. Now the dominant song of joy and happiness is drowned out by Kino's manic desire to keep the pearl at any price, even murder. His readiness to kill in order to keep the treasure leads to the first verbal recognition and admission of the gem's duality. Again an ironic twist is used as Juana, unlike her biblical counterpart Eve, is the first to see the dark elements in the pearl.

Yet despite his wife's warning, Kino persists in seeing only one side of the pearl, and consequently only one side of his human nature. He refuses to acknowledge how inextricably good is mixed with evil, light with darkness, and harmony with dissonance, nor does he see the pearl and the scorpion as similar. Indeed, the vague wavering of Kino's mind about the subject is suggested as the narrator pictures the pearl as "winking and glimmering in the light of the little candle, cozening Kino's brain with its beauty."

Later, when Kino's brother Juan Thomas tries to reason with him, he suggests the futility of trying to obtain a fair price from the pearl buyers in the town, where there is a further duplicity: a cheating monopoly of merchants who pose as agents of free enterprise but who are in fact defrauding their customers and controlling the prices in the pearl market for their own personal gain.

Nonetheless Kino persists in his refusal to listen to and recognize duality, still preferring to believe in a rigid code of good and evil which is applicable to all men, and not to just a select few. Such a code is not vague or hazy in nature but upright and constantly just and honest. Obviously this idealistic code is unattainable, and Kino's belief in it is destroyed when the pearl buyers assert that the pearl's size makes it only a curiosity—clumsy, undesirable, and of less worth.

KINO'S DEGRADATION

This act of trickery infuriates Kino, and Steinbeck repeats his association with the pearl as Kino becomes tighter and harder rather than more pliable. As [critic] Todd Lieber notes, the pearl is "a complex talisman, containing Steinbeck's vision of man: it is a thing of great worth and beauty and promise, but it also appears cancerous and ugly; it evokes avarice and greed, but also generosity and kindness; it produces high and noble thoughts and ambition, but also theft and murder. Steinbeck had come to believe that good and evil were inseparable from being, intimately related parts of that which is."

Lieber, however, fails to note Kino's intense identification with the talisman and how the evil of the pearl coagulates about its victim, entrapping him with its glistening yet deadly light. Consequently, Kino is as helpless in its throes as he is before the deceiving pearl buyers. Like the townspeople, his only solution is to lie to himself, for admitting the duplicity around him would force both Kino and his friends to acknowledge the lengthy amount of time that they have allowed themselves to be duped.

The dark music returns to Kino's life as he refuses the offer of monopoly for the Pearl of Great Price, but the evil melody is still countered and balanced by Juana's Song of the Family, which restores safety, warmth, and wholeness at

least momentarily. However, shortly thereafter Juana re-
states her mistrust in the treasure: "Kino," she says, "the
pearl is evil. Let us destroy it before it destroys us. Let us
crush it between stones. Let us—let us throw it back in the
sea where it belongs! Kino, it is evil, it is evil!!"

Sadly, Kino again ignores the warning, this time asserting
that the qualities of his masculinity—determination and inge-
nuity—will serve as proof against evil. What he fails to recognize is that the dark side of these qualities—stubbornness and
craftiness—have also infiltrated his life. In order to attain the
self-insight about moral ambiguity that he so desperately
needs, Steinbeck forces Kino to face death itself. Nothing less
than physical death is required to transcend or cope with his
fallen nature. It is the price a person must pay to discover his
true identity. Each one must give birth to himself, then die of
the consequences. To be human is to know death.

DARK FORCES

Kino's ensuing fight with Juana emphasizes the separation,
dissonance, and darkness in their relationship that have
been caused by the questionable treasure. Kino becomes
more domineering and greedy, and in a short while he is
forced to commit murder as well as battery in order to retain
the pearl. After this, the powers of evil seem to concentrate
on an absolute destruction of Kino's life. In a way it is a punishment for his unwillingness to accept the ambiguous nature of the pearl and for his determination to see it as an absolute. The now-dominant dark force destroys Kino's canoe
(his life source) and his brush home and eventually seeks
even his life. As Kino reflects on the shifting nature of everything around him, he recognizes, like [Joseph] Conrad's
Kurtz in *Heart of Darkness*, that "it is all darkness—all darkness and the shape of darkness." Yet, like Kurtz, he must
pursue his life though it causes him misfortune, and he must
seek his goals though they bring about his own destruction.
His self-identification with duality is complete as he states,
"The Pearl has become my soul. If I give it up, I shall lose my
soul." Kino's life has been transformed; he is totally the opposite of what he was at the novel's beginning.

The only option for Juana and Kino now is flight, and like
Adam and Eve they are evicted from their Eden into a hostile world complete with an unfriendly wind and cold, un-
caring stars in a black sky. Like man's first parents, they

mistrust one another, and the oneness of their marriage in the early chapters is replaced by separation and selfishness. Returning to the sight imagery, Steinbeck notes that the joy which was previously held in the light has been transformed into Kino's revelry in death and destruction and the ways of the dark. The sound image also returns: "the music of the pearl was triumphant in Kino's head and the quiet melody of the family underlay it." This positive picture is, of course, ironic, and it suggests that despite the bitter trials which his newfound wealth has brought, Kino still persists in his belief that the pearl's dual nature must be illusory. Though its evil glow burns in his eyes, he sees his bad luck as emanating from elsewhere than his treasure, and, ironically, he still seeks his vision in its surface.

When he once again consults the pearl's surface for answers, the magic crystal ball reveals that his own goals have been twisted and warped. The power of the rifle has become murder, the ecstasy of religious faith and commitment have become spouse abuse, and the value of an educated child has been transformed into illness and even death. As [critic Lester] Marks notes, "The courageous and trusting Kino experiences for the first time in his life the emotions of defensive fear and suspicion, and in his blindness he courts destruction of all he values most. His vain struggle to protect the pearl brings about the loss of his home, a spiritual estrangement from his wife and the death of his son."

Stubbornly Kino rejects the evil vision, but as he thrusts the pearl into his clothing, the sound images remind him that the Music of the Pearl has become sinister in his ears and is interwoven with the music of evil. At this point the novel again poses the premise that in order to overcome evil, man's duality must be acknowledged rather than hidden or ignored. Failure to do so only results in a hell on earth, and so it is for Kino.

FLIGHT

As he and Juana flee desperately toward the mountains, they discover only [T.S.] Eliot's Waste Land—waterless desert covered with cacti and sharp rocks. This is a sharp contrast from the biblical promise "I will lift up my eyes to the hills from whence cometh my help" (Psalms 121:1), and it is yet another ironic reversal which suggests the duality that infects man's world. These hell-like surroundings encourage the dual musical image to return, and it is described as loud, hot, secret, and poisonous. The symbols of the pearl (originally positive) and the scorpion (originally negative) are now joined as Kino's existence becomes that of all postlapsarian Adams. He is drawn simultaneously toward "good" and "evil," which often are intertwined and inseparable.

Kino instinctively heads for a cleft in a rock and the safety symbolized by caves, water, and valleys in Steinbeck's other fiction. But despite the family's arrival at a supposed place of protection, there is still the potential for death and destruction. Like the pearl, the water and the cave have two faces, and the reader senses that both may signal death and destruction rather than resurrection and new life. The reader is again drawn to Steinbeck's musical imagery as Kino fights for his life. Suddenly the Song of the Family, previously peaceful and harmonic, has been changed into a sharp battle cry. Ironically, in order to attain a good for himself and his family, Kino must again resort to evil: the dark deed of murder.

Eventually he succeeds in his rescue plans, but darkness is essential to his attempt, and his efforts are marred by the light of the moon. On the third try, however, he is successful in killing all three of the dark riders who have pursued them. But this apparent victory is short-lived as he discovers that a random shot has struck the top of Coyotito's head, killing him instantly. The sacrifice of the firstborn son, a recurring concern in at least three other Steinbeck novels, brings Kino to his senses even as it awakened Abraham, the Israelites in Egypt, and believers in Christ Jesus.

KNOWLEDGE OF THE PEARL

After Coyotito's death, Juana and Kino seem removed from the present, and they are transformed into archetypes. The narrator, however, emphasizes the positive rather than the negative side of the experience: "They had gone through pain and had come out on the other side; that there was almost a magical protection about them." Kino now has a new and more accurate vision of the pearl. "He looked into its surface and it was gray and ulcerous. Evil faces peered from it into his eyes, and he saw the light of burning. And in the surface he saw the frantic eyes of the man lying in the pool. And in the surface of the pearl he saw Coyotito lying in the little cave with the top of his head shot away. And the pearl was ugly; it was gray, like a malignant growth. And Kino heard the music of the pearl, distorted and insane."

With this knowledge the relationship of Juana and Kino is restored; both now possess a complete awareness of the pearl's double nature. This change is indicated by the fact that when they return to La Paz, they walk not in single file but side by side, and when Kino throws the pearl into the water, they remain side by side for a long time. This return to unity suggests a catharsis and redemption, a return from the valley of the shadow of death. In fact, as the novel draws to a close, it appears as if Kino and Juana have traveled full circle and found renewed unity even in the darkness. "The sun was behind them and their long shadows stalked ahead, and they seemed to carry two towers of darkness with them."

As the novel returns to its initial setting of mixed light and dark, Steinbeck indicates man's inescapable condition. In the final pages, Kino has matured; he has accepted the duality of all things. As [critic] Harry Morris points out, Kino and Juana are doubles of Everyman, who in his journey toward death discovers who he really is.

> The full significance of Kino's throwing the pearl back into the sea now becomes clear: the act represents the willingness to accept a third journey, the journey still to be made, the journey that any fictional character has still to make after his dream-vision allegory is over. . . . They must apply their new knowledge and win their way to eternal salvation, which can only come with their actual deaths. But his real triumph, his real gain, the heights to which he has risen rather than the depths to which he has slipped back is the immense knowledge he has gained of good and evil. This knowledge is the tool that he needs to help him on the final journey, the inescapable journey that Everyman must take.

A sadder but wiser Kino now faces his former existence with knowledge and intuition. He will never be the same, and neither will the sensitive reader who has accompanied him on his journey. In fact, this reader will be forced, like the protagonist, to examine his soul and to deny the lack of moral absolutes. Perhaps he will even agree with Steinbeck that "if this story is a parable, perhaps everyone takes his own meaning from it and reads his own life into it." Whatever that meaning, the careful crafting of imagery (sight, sound, and symbols) reveals that Steinbeck's novella is indeed a complex tale which not only possesses archetypal significance but which, when examined closely, offers a deep moral lesson to conscientious readers.

The Pearl: A Parable of Hope

Charles R. Metzger

"And they began this day with hope." So Steinbeck ends chapter 3 of *The Pearl*, signifying, according to Charles R. Metzger, an onslaught of trouble for the protagonist Kino. Metzger observes that through Kino, Steinbeck demonstrates the high price man can pay for hoping: At the beginning of the novel, Kino is surviving at the barest subsistence level, without hope for a better life yet relatively content with his meager condition. Discovery of the pearl arouses hope in Kino, who envisions the wealth and security that the pearl will bring. This hopeful thinking, coupled with a stubborn refusal to accept his station in life and fear of hope thwarted, propels Kino on a perilous course that ultimately costs him the life of his only son. Metzger contributed this article to *Research Studies*, a journal of the University of Southern California.

In the headnote to his 1947 version of *The Pearl*, John Steinbeck suggests that his story ought to be considered a parable. "If," he writes, "this story is a parable, perhaps everyone takes his own meaning from it . . . and reads his own life into it." I think it is worthwhile to consider the possibility that Steinbeck himself, during the very processes of thinking about the story and of writing it, may have given his own meaning to the story, may have written his own life into it.

It so happens that the portion of Steinbeck's own life which comes closest in time and place to his parable of *The Pearl* is rather carefully recorded in *The Log from the Sea of Cortez*, namely the period during the spring of 1940 when Steinbeck and Ed Ricketts were quite self-consciously combining the scientific collecting of marine animals from the

Excerpted from Charles R. Metzger, "Steinbeck's *The Pearl* as a Nonteleological Parable of Hope," *Research Studies*, vol. 46 (June 1978). Reprinted by permission of the author.

littoral [coastal region] of the Gulf of California with romantic adventure. In the middle of chapter 11 of *The Log*, dated
March 20, 1940, Steinbeck reports the story of an Indian boy
near La Paz who "by accident found a pearl of great size, an
unbelievable pearl." Steinbeck then goes on to comment:
"This seems to be a true story, but it is so much like a parable that it almost can't be. This Indian boy is too heroic, too
wise. He knows too much and acts on his knowledge. In
every way, he goes contrary to human direction. This story
is probably true, but we don't believe it; it is far too reasonable to be true.". . .

And it is in these same chapters, more specifically chapters 10, 14, and 16, that he says most of what he has to say . . .
about hope as a human mutation, and about the statistically
small chance of any survival value developing out of mutation in general and of hope as a mutation in particular.

What I propose is to consider seriously what Steinbeck
had to say in *The Log* regarding the nature of human
thought and human truth regarding [hope as a human] mutation and its survival value, these insofar as Steinbeck's and
Ricketts' and their crew's speculations concerning such
matters appear to shed light upon what is going on in Steinbeck's parable of *The Pearl*.

What happened, apparently, in the time of Steinbeck's life
during which he was exposed not only to the original pearl
story but also to the physical and social circumstances of the
natives who told it, was that Steinbeck and Ricketts and the
crew of the *Western Flyer* began to think about the natives
around La Paz, and ultimately about all men, using the
modes of thought that they themselves were using daily in
thinking about marine animals. As ecologists they were concerned with observing marine animals in their total environment. Although their immediate focus of attention was
always upon the animals surrounding a particular collecting
station, sometimes those within a given tide pool, their general mode of thought was expansive and speculative, limited
only by the personal character of each observer and by the
vigor and keenness of his mind. "A man looking [thus] at reality," observed Steinbeck, "brings his own limitations to
[that] world. If he has strength and energy of mind the tide
pool stretches both ways, digs back to electrons and leaps
space into the universe and fights out of the moment into
non-conceptual time. Then ecology has a synonym which is

ALL." Near the end of *The Log* Steinbeck reported, more or less in summary of their efforts: "We tried always to understand that the reality we observed was partly us; the speculations, our product."

NONTELEOLOGICAL THINKING

Theirs was . . . a relatively new way of thinking, deriving from close observation initially of how things *are*, phenomenally, in all of their sometimes-complex relationships. It is a way of thinking which holds "conscious acceptance [of the way things are] as a desideratum, . . . as an all-important prerequisite" to speculative thought. Steinbeck called such thinking nonteleological, or "is" thinking, which he said, "concerns itself *primarily* not with what should be, or could be, or might be, but rather with what actually 'is'—attempting at most to answer the already sufficiently difficult questions *what* and *how*, instead of *why*."

Such thinking does not rule out considerations regarding cause so much as it attempts to take into account man's lust for causal explanations, explanations that are often conditioned more by simple hope for a favorable change than by recognition of the often-complex relationships between things as they are. "It is amazing," wrote Steinbeck, "how the strictures of the old teleologies infect our observation, causal thinking warped by hope." Such hope, he had suggested earlier, has the quality of "a diagnostic trait. . . . For hope implies a change from a present bad condition to a future better one." Thus infected by hope, Kino in *The Pearl* envisions an improved time when he will have a new harpoon, a rifle, shoes and new clothing for his family, have his marriage sanctified by the church, education for his son, all of these in consequence of the accident of having discovered the pearl.

Such "teleological thinking," Steinbeck continues in *The Log*, "is most frequently associated with the evaluating [the diagnosing] of cause and effect, the purposiveness [not the accidentalness] of events. This thinking considers changes and cures—what 'should be' in terms of an end pattern: it presumes the bettering of conditions, often, unfortunately, without achieving more than a most superficial understanding of those conditions." Notions born of such thinking become harmfully infectious, Steinbeck continues, when "in their sometimes intolerant refusal to face facts as they are, teleological notions may substitute a fierce but ineffectual attempt to change conditions which are assumed to be undesirable, in place of the understanding-acceptance which would pave the way for a more sensible attempt at any change which might still be indicated."

In *The Pearl* Steinbeck demonstrates this kind of refusal to face facts in Kino's stubborn resistance to being cheated out of the pearl, even though he has been accustomed to being cheated all of his life. This stubborn refusal to face facts increases through stages of progressive aggravation and developing fear (which is the silent partner of hope) until Kino has killed at least four men and has lost by accident, and despite his desperate maneuverings, the life of his son, even as by accident he originally found the great pearl.

RELINQUISHING HOPE

It takes Kino a good deal longer, in the face of much harsher provocation, to "catch on," than it did the original, incredible, Indian boy of La Paz. And it does so, in part, because Kino is less capable of that understanding-acceptance, characterized in *The Pearl* by his brother Juan Tomás and the Indian boy of La Paz. Kino surrenders hope of earthly reward to be derived from the pearl only after the most severe depredations on account of it. For his part the Indian boy is merely beaten and tortured. He does not lose his house, his canoe, his son. He is not tracked down to be killed.

At the beginning of Steinbeck's parable Kino and Juana are living successfully without hope at the subsistence level. Kino has a boat, assuring them food and such pearls as Kino can find. These provide what little cash they get. They have a house, as good as any other native house. They have a son, evidence of their masculinity and femininity, their biological maturity, their ability to reproduce. Such crises as occur, as in the case of the scorpion sting, Kino faces instinctively, nonverbally, effectively, without plans.

It is with hope that the trouble really begins, trouble that cannot be dealt with without verbalizing, without planning. It is not by accident that Steinbeck ends chapter 3 of *The Pearl* with this single sentence referring to Kino and Juana: "And they began this day with hope."

Steinbeck suggests in *The Log* that there are two principal kinds of hopeful, or teleological, thought: spiritual and physical. "Spiritual teleology," he says, "is rare" nowadays. It is significant in this connection that Kino's hope regarding matters spiritual and religious is different from the original Indian boy's. Kino wishes merely to have his and Juana's union recognized, made socially respectable, by the church. The Indian boy wished to purchase quick exit from Purgatory after death for himself as well as for a "number of his dead relatives."

It is largely this secular kind of teleology, of hopeful thinking, which is physical and materialistic rather than spiritual, that is aroused in Kino, and present also in the physician, and in the members of the pearl buyers' association. As Steinbeck suggests in *The Log*, we live today, most of us, within a materialistic, technologically oriented frame of reference largely conditioned by hope.

Yet this very concern with material things, with technology, is for the most part unnecessary to mere biological survival. It is man's desire, his hope, suggests Steinbeck, that has created technology and "technical ability." "Physiologically," he observes, "man does not require this paraphernalia to exist." But, he adds immediately, "*the whole man* does. He is the only animal who lives outside himself, whose drive is in external things—property, houses, money, concepts of power . . . [and once] having projected himself into these external complexities, he *is* them. His house, his automobile are a part of him and a large part of him."

I should like to suggest that Kino is like ourselves, and therefore credible to us, insofar as he cares about his burned house, his ruined Nayarit canoe, and cherishes his tools and weapons. Yet for both the man living at the barest subsistence level and the man living amidst the material abundance of things which a technology born of hope provides him as projections of himself, the basic problem remains the same for each, as it does for marine animals between tides, namely, survival. Without survival there is no time, no individual, no species, most certainly no concern with cause—there is no drive, either warped or regulated by hope. "There would seem to be only one commandment for living things," wrote Steinbeck in *The Log*. It is: "Survive!"

THE THEME OF SURVIVAL

Survival, I suggest, is a major theme also in *The Pearl*. Its importance is announced by Juan Tomás, Kino's wiser, older brother. And what Juan Tomás announces Kino learns and demonstrates, almost not surviving, in the process, his lesson by ordeal. Juan Tomás is a much more important character in *The Pearl* than is generally recognized. For one thing he provides expository information to Kino and the reader. He tells what has happened in the past to other natives who entertained the hope of selling their pearls at a fair price, and then acted upon that hope, with fatal consequences. But his function is larger. It is choral as well as expository, inasmuch as Juan Tomás announces the theme of survival. "We do know," he says, "that we are cheated from birth to overcharge on our coffins. *But we survive.*"

Juan Tomás not only tells Kino and the reader what the basic issue is, but he also helps Kino in realistic ways to survive. He not only gives Kino important information that Kino does not know, he not only gives him important advice, but he hides Kino and his family as long as it is safe to do so, broadcasting misleading suggestions as to where Kino might have gone. He collects food and water for Kino and his family, and provides Kino with the "great work knife," with which Kino is finally able to kill quickly two of the three pursuers who are trying to kill him.

Even as Juan Tomás announces the theme of survival, Kino demonstrates it, not only at the biological level of animal subsistence, but at the more human level to which he is transported by the complications which attend his entertaining hope. At the beginning of Steinbeck's *The Pearl*, Kino is surviving at a bare subsistence level, without hope. For example, he has lost his iron harpoon. But having no hope of getting another one, he makes do without it. He lives not entirely without a measure of fear, but the fear he experiences is nonteleological, instinctual. He knows which plants and animals are poisonous or otherwise dangerous, and he avoids them. He recognizes the scorpion as an enemy nonverbally, as suggested by the Song of the Enemy. He is living, incredibly to us, without aspirations, without plans, i.e., without hope.

FEAR OF HOPE THWARTED

After he discovers the great pearl Kino lives constantly *with* hope and with a new kind of fear, fear of hope thwarted. This is the modern fear, as Steinbeck suggests repeatedly throughout his work, that plagues all but the most exceptional of modern men. In a most vividly parabolic sense Kino demonstrates what a high price a man can pay for hoping. For in embracing hope a man comes inevitably into conflict with other men's hopes and the fears attending them, including among many men fear of change in the status quo, to match the opposing fear that the status quo will not be changed. Hence the fierce, occasionally mortal contests regarding the question of whose hopes are to be realized and whose hopes are to be frustrated.

Kino's innocent hope of selling his fabulous pearl for a fabulous price causes ultimately five deaths. Insofar as Kino demonstrates that even the least-motivated man cannot, by virtue of accident, entirely escape becoming involved in entertaining and therefore needing hope, he also demonstrates that, as an emerging "whole man" in Steinbeck's terms, he has to learn to live with hope, to pay the price for so doing, when he must, and to refuse to pay the price for entertaining hope when it becomes evident, as it usually does after the fact, that the price has been too high. This kind of accounting has perhaps at least as much survival value, Steinbeck suggests, even for the marginally hopeful man, as other less-verbal kinds of instinct.

Steinbeck suggests in *The Log* that hope in man may be a form of mutation distinguishing him from other animals. Mutation, Steinbeck recognizes, is bittersweet in terms of survival value, inasmuch as biological mutation has generally very low, even negative, survival value. Accordingly, hope as a mutation could easily lead, when statistically considered, to self-destruction. In Kino's case it almost does. The fact that it does not is crucially important. As the parable ends, Kino has learned, the hard way, the high price of hope. He has paid the price—perhaps too high a price—but he has survived. And he returns to cast the pearl back into the sea, armed, not only with the Winchester rifle, the only thing he had hoped for that he actually got, but armed with a newly sophisticated awareness of what hope costs—of how low-yield are the rewards of hope as a mutation. But he does survive as did the original Indian boy. And this outcome is important to the parable.

The Pearl: A Novel of Disengagement

Tetsumaro Hayashi

Steinbeck scholar Tetsumaro Hayashi explains how *The Pearl* operates as a novel of disengagement on two levels: first, Kino's purposeful withdrawal from his place in the natural scheme, and later his renouncement of the pearl. Indeed, the lure of the pearl blinds Kino's spiritual vision and causes him to disengage from his simple—yet content—life. Only the devastating loss of his son counteracts the contaminating effects of the pearl. Through a second disengagement, this time from the pearl, Kino ultimately finds salvation and peace of mind.

John Steinbeck's *The Pearl* (1947) can properly be called the novel of disengagement on at least two levels, for it traces the symbolic journey and withdrawal of the novel's protagonist, Kino, first from the environment of society, his family, and even from his own proper place in the natural scheme; and, secondly, from the charm of the Pearl of the World. The first withdrawal is best seen as the misguided alienation from everything that gives life spiritual value and moral direction; the second is best seen as the recognition of the pearl as a symbol of the perverse greed inherent in the scheme of things which, like the scorpion's poison, can infect an otherwise healthy organism, such as Kino's being and that of his family.

The novel operates on two levels, then, and draws its dynamic flow from a recurrent process of commitment to false values and a later disengagement from them. The pearl, thus, is not the means to freedom, with its promises of wealth, pride, respect, status, and hope for his family; in reality it is a self-discovered poison and the visible symbol not of material poverty, but of moral bankruptcy, not of salva-

From Tetsumaro Hayashi, "*The Pearl* as the Novel of Disengagement," *Steinbeck Quarterly*, Summer/Fall 1974. Reprinted by permission of the *Steinbeck Quarterly*.

tion but of the inherent "heart of darkness" dormant in every human breast. It takes *Gedatsu* [total disengagement or extrication in Zen philosophy], the total disengagement from this magnificent obsession, to save him from the curse of the Pearl of the World. The face of evil, here and everywhere, is at first brilliant, attractive, and tempting. It is only natural, then, that when Kino first discovers the pearl, he is deceived by its brilliance and the false promise it holds out to him. His fascination with the pearl becomes so great, in fact, that it soon becomes his total obsession, completely upsetting his scale of values, displacing his sense of filial and social community, and even consuming his moral sense. Thus he declares that "This pearl has become my soul. If I give it up, I shall lose my soul." An obsessed man, Kino embraces false values and equates the symbol of material wealth with the soul.

DEADLY OBSESSION

Kino's faith in the seemingly desirable nature of the pearl is no less than an obsession, an obsession made with almost religious fervor, as the pearl becomes Kino's new God. This allegorical shift is expressed by Steinbeck's favorite device, namely, the literary "montage" which gives the reader a dual image of the pearl as a thematic focus. It is still true, nevertheless, that the pearl is at one point Kino's dream of the future and his indulgence in an elevated new status in society. Yet the same object, so priceless and so beautiful, symbolizes a false sense of value that blinds Kino and so many other men and prompts them to become evil-minded, greedy, fearful, and destructive. The pearl buyers, the doctor, and their agents, become "slaves of passion," no doubt; but Kino joins their company in prizing what they value. The pearl, as a mammon [possession with a debasing influence], appears to be a "Life Force," and yet it is an allegory of Death. Therefore, the possessor of the pearl is in reality possessed by its charm; he is at once blessed and cursed, owner and slave, freed from poverty but chained to his enemies.

Ironically enough, the pearl is bound to destroy its possessor and all those who covet it. And yet Kino, like those who are enslaved by avarice, temporarily loses his spiritual vision until he loses his real "Pearl" in the world: his only son, Coyotito. Like Mr. Kurtz in Joseph Conrad's *Heart of Darkness*, whose soul is possessed by the ivory and his lust for it, Kino is possessed by the pearl and his obsession with it. And, lifeless God now has a mysterious dual image: the image of life and the simultaneous image of death. Kino does not fully recognize its duality until his son is shot to death by one of the pursuers. Then in the pearl can he clearly see the dual image: the "frantic eyes of the man (Kino killed) in the pool" and "Coyotito lying in the little cave with the top of his head shot away." Ironically, the name "Coyotito" means "little Coyote" in Spanish, and the boy is thus perhaps not only a son but a symbol of the living force in nature condemned to be the victim of the predatory instinct in man.

However, through his *Gedatsu*, Kino learns to face his Fate when he is chased by the invisible pursuers. When he is convinced that there is "no exit," he experiences Hamlet's *Satori* [awakening or illumination in Zen philosophy] as exemplified by the Prince's ultimate concerns: "The readiness is all" and "Let it be." Kino, like Prince Hamlet, recognizes that he would have to face his Fate sooner or later, and the only way to find the way from bondage to freedom is to confront Fate with courage and dignity. As Kino experiences this *Satori*, his Great Illumination, he is able to extricate himself from the self-discovered prison: the Pearl of the World, the false promise and deceptive mammon.

As his brother Juan Thomas once warns, Kino has "defied the whole structure" by rejecting the deceptive prices the pearl buyers offered; Kino thus defies the whole material society: the group of pearl buyers, the doctor, and their agents of avarice, and all other evil men in the society who have their own strong will independent of Kino's. Since he had read some of D.H. Lawrence's work, Steinbeck may well have known that for Lawrence the name John Thomas, which Steinbeck converts to Spanish, symbolizes the instinctive forces of nature. It is significant to note also that Juana, Kino's wife, instinctively detects the evil nature of the pearl, which has blinded Kino's spiritual vision almost completely.

AN INESCAPABLE FATE

The pearl appears beautiful, priceless, and desirable all at once, but Juana knows that it is contrary to all of these apparent qualities which deceive Kino and those who covet it. In fact, she even tries in vain to throw the pearl away just to save her husband from disaster and self-destruction and to free Kino from this magnificent obsession with the evil pearl. However, when Kino defiantly tells her, "I am a man," she knows exactly what he means by that: he is "half insane" and "half god." Juana knows also that as "half insane and half divine" Kino would "dare to fight with the highest mountain and plunge his strength against the sea." Hereafter she unconditionally supports Kino's efforts to escape the pursuers, or rather, to face them, not only because she loves him but also because she understands her husband and his inescapable Fate. It is almost as if she knew that man's destiny is to embrace what is harmful to him, to covet what is wrong, and to prepare his own poison. Like Teiresias in Sophocles's *Oedipus Rex*, she lets the protagonist weave the net of his own future.

As soon as Kino starts an undeclared war against the absurd society of pearl buyers, the doctor, and their agents, the enemies immediately try to kill Kino and his family and to steal his pearl. Discovering the pearl, therefore, turns out to be like tasting the Forbidden Fruit. Like Adam and Eve, Kino and Juana have to be banished from the Eden-like society after they are exposed to the secret knowledge of evil through the Pearl of the World; ultimately, this proves to be "Fortunate Fall," for Kino finally experiences his *Satori*. After his discovery there will continuously be a vicious circle around Kino; the more he protects the ownership of the pearl, the more exposed he is to the dangers of invisible enemies. Kino cannot find his peace of mind until he disengages himself totally from his magnificent obsession with the pearl, the very source that contaminates him. The pearl, like the evil king in the Elizabethan world who spiritually pollutes the kingdom, contaminates Kino's soul anal attempts to destroy his tie with the village and nature where he, though poor, would find happiness, peace, harmony, and love.

RENOUNCING THE PEARL

However, Coyotito's death forces him to recognize the illusion he has taken as a reality; his son's sudden death is a kind of sacrifice to a pagan god Kino has blindly and fanatically worshipped; this painful experience restores Kino's sanity and vision. At long last Kino is able to recognize the naked truth: the pearl will never insure his future, but destroy it. He regains a kind of stability and vision that makes him recognize the truth, that the only way to be saved is to be without the pearl, without the obsession: specifically, it is through the equally magnificent *disengagement* from the mammon, that he can achieve his salvation. This means that a total self-negation gives him subdued but enduring freedom from bondage and fear and that he now is able to face his future and to discover a new purpose in the otherwise "absurd and cruel" society. He has looked into the evil . . . not only in others but in himself, and withdrawn from that confrontation with a darker being within himself; thus he becomes aware of the true nature of man and his lonely Fate.

It is this *Satori* that brings Kino and Juana back to their village; there is something inviolable about them when they quietly walk through the village. There is no fear, no obsession, no anger. By throwing the Pearl of the World back into the sea, Kino has regained his peace, security, and most importantly, his natural tie with the village. He is once again able to live there, not as an alienated figure, but as a citizen of his own community, which is his only reality. Paradoxically speaking, he restores his real being by totally renouncing his false being. Thus Steinbeck's *The Pearl*, the novel of disengagement, tells us the very painful but noteworthy journey of Kino's *Gedatsu* and *Satori*, which finally teaches him the way to bring himself from bondage to freedom, from fear to fearlessness, and from Death to Rebirth. He restores himself by means of his total self-negation.

Thematic Structure in *The Pearl*

Ernest E. (Ernie) Karsten Jr.

The Pearl opens with Kino surrounded by his family, basking in security, warmth, and love. Ernest E. Karsten Jr. (now more widely known as Ernie Karsten) proposes that *The Pearl* is Steinbeck's exploration of man's existence in the context of these and other human relationships, which give life meaning. Karsten explores two manifestations of this central theme: Specifically, Steinbeck uses music— the Song of the Family, the Song of the Pearl, and the Song of Evil—to parallel the book's human relationships. Secondly, Steinbeck's masterful descriptions illustrate human relationships within Kino's community and also the parasitic relationship between that community and the town. Karsten, a former high school teacher, contributed the following critical essay to a 1965 edition of *English Journal.*

As a simple story well told and at the same time a complicated work of art well constructed, John Steinbeck's *The Pearl* has long been a work popular with students in secondary school and college. The combination of simple story, strongly established symbolism, social commentary, and important themes, as well as beautiful writing, makes this a literary work that may well become a classic and certainly as fine an introduction to the genre as could be found.

Our purpose here is to deal with thematic material: to define a few of what are the major ideas in the novel and to trace them through the structure of the plot. Well aware of the author's admonition that "everyone takes his own meaning" from this story, we do not claim omniscience. We hope, however, that this discussion of theme and structure will be helpful to each individual's interpreting and appreciating this novel and provide additional insights for those who may *teach* it.

Before advancing to thematic material, it may be well to establish immediately what we hold as the structure of the novel. Although the structure could be shown schematically, let us use words. Each chapter contains a central incident which has both cause and effect, tying together the action. In Chapter I the central incident is accidental, the scorpion's stinging Coyotito, and results in the need to find a pearl with which to pay for a doctor's treatment. The discovery of the pearl, the fruit of purposeful action for something good and the central incident of Chapter II, has the effect of making Kino everyone's enemy, the townspeople's becoming a threat to Kino and his family. Chapters III and IV have as central incidents the attacks upon Kino for possession of the pearl. These attacks are both physical as well as emotional (the doctor's "treatment" of Coyotito) or intellectual (the pearl buyer's attempt to take advantage of Kino's ignorance), and they arise from a human evil, greed. These incidents result in the growing conflict between Kino and Juana over the pearl. In Chapter V the turning point is reached in the central incident of that chapter, the destruction of what we call *existence* for Kino, caused by purposeful action for an evil goal. The effect of this incident is Kino's forced emigration from the community. The central incident of the final chapter is the death of Coyotito, again, as in the first chapter, an accidental incident, which results in Kino's return to the community and the destruction of the pearl.

THE PEARL'S CENTRAL THEME

With this structure in mind, let us turn now to the central theme. Just as the pearl is an "accident," so is man's existence, and that existence has meaning within human relationships, basic of which is the family. Just as the pearl is good or becomes invested with evil because of the ways men use it, so man himself appears, becomes, emerges as good or evil because of the ways men use other men, nurturing or destroying the human relationship between them, validating or invalidating the meaning of their existence.

We have attempted to trace two manifestations of this theme through the novel. The first follows Steinbeck's use of music as a symbolic representation of the theme paralleling the basic story. The second manifestation is found in Stein-

beck's use of description to suggest the relationships between Kino and his community and between the community
and the town as social embodiments of the theme again paralleling the basic story.

   Steinbeck has established three main songs that are
named: the Songs of the Family, of Evil, and of the Pearl.
Schematically, these three melodies can be envisioned as
originating on three separate planes, with the Song of the
Family in the middle and the Song of Evil on a parallel
plane, but imminent. From a plane below both, the Song of
the Pearl is created and, as the story itself progresses, moves
forward to become one with the Song of the Family, then to
transcend it and join with the Song of Evil.

STEINBECK'S USE OF MUSIC

Within the first few pages two songs are heard: the Song of
the Family is identified along with other unnamed songs,
the heritage of Kino's people, in the calm beginning of the
story; the Song of Evil is heard for the first time with the attack of the scorpion and later as the music of the enemy
when Kino stands before the doctor's house. During the
search for a pearl, the Song of the Pearl is being given birth
by the Songs of the Undersea and of the Pearl That Might Be,
then is finally heard clearly and richly as Kino holds the
pearl in his hand. Later in the story, when Kino and his
pearl are the center of attention in his hut, the Songs of the
Family and of the Pearl harmonize; but with the coming of
the priest and then of awareness of his vulnerability Kino
again hears the Song of Evil, which continues to be heard intermittently through the doctor's visits to the first attack.
Again, when Kino senses the dishonesty of the pearl buyer,
the Song of Evil is heard and reappears during the second attack. During Chapter V, the Song of the Family is completely
interrupted while the Song of Evil is omnipresent. At the beginning of the emigration, the Song of the Pearl is triumphant over the re-established Song of the Family but
soon becomes sinister and merges with the Song of Evil.
During the flight from the trackers, the Song of Evil (the
Pearl) is loudly heard until Kino, at bay, decides to attack.
Then the Song of the Family becomes a snarl, and finally a
battle cry until the distorted Song of the Pearl is silenced.

   As symbolic representation, the musical parallel must
now be related to the central theme. Within the human rela-

tionship where Kino's life has meaning, the Song of the Family is warm, clear, soft, and protecting. Herein the Song of the Family represents completeness. It continues to have these qualities as long as the Song of the Pearl does not overwhelm it. As Steinbeck writes, "they beautify one another." When the human relationship is threatened and destroyed (the crisis: Juana attempts to toss away the pearl, Kino strikes her, Kino is attacked and commits murder, Juana realizes the irrevocable change and accepts it to keep the family together, and the change is manifested in the destruction of the old ties of boat and home, and the pearl becomes both life and soul for Kino), the Song of the Family is interrupted and then becomes secondary to the Song of the Pearl. But because life's meaning is now dependent upon the pearl rather than upon human relationships, the Song of the Pearl becomes the Song of Evil opposed to the Song of the Family, which is now harsh, snarling, and defensive—a fierce cry until the Song of the Pearl is stilled and the human relationships are restored within the original community.

SUGGESTIVE IMAGES

Through the suggestive power of Steinbeck's description, the second manifestation of the theme becomes clear: the close harmony in the human relationships within Kino's community and the parasitic relationship between that community and the town. Within the first few pages, Steinbeck presents a pair of descriptive phrases which he will continue to use in order to strengthen the reader's image of the relationships already mentioned. He juxtaposes the "brush houses" of the community and the "stone and plaster houses" of the town. This basic image suggests several ideas. Perhaps the first is the idea of impermanence on the one hand and solidity on the other. Life for the community is a precarious as well as a precious thing, subject not only to the whims of Fate but to the demands of the town, its needs and wants; the town, however, has the strength to withstand Chance and to endure.

Steinbeck elaborates upon his description of the town. He progresses from the "stone and plaster houses" to the phrase "city of stone and plaster," and further to "the city of harsh outer walls and inner cool gardens where a little water played and the bougainvillaea crusted the walls with purple, brick-red, and white," and finally to "the secret gardens . . . the singing of caged birds . . . and the splash of cooling water on hot flagstones." Later he repeats the images by referring to the wall, water, and caged birds.

The images of the "secret gardens," "caged birds," and fountains bespeak verdant and cool beauty beneath a relentless sun. What could be more desirable? Or natural? Yet, if these images are suggestive of human relationships, of the juxtaposed modes of life, their normalcy must be questioned. Thus, as "stone and plaster houses" suggests a retreat from the vital contest, so too do these images suggest a refuge. Moreover, they are unnatural. A "secret garden" is the property of one who cannot appreciate nature's garden wherever it may be, primarily it would seem, because nature's garden is not his alone. Similarly, a "caged bird" is only a substitute for the melodies so naturally a part of Kino's people, and a fountain is a poor imitation of the lullaby of the sea. These images at first thought are completely acceptable; but, when questioned, they corroborate the picture of the town as protective and withdrawn from life and nature and suggest that the people are almost as lifeless and unnatural as their gardens.

In the phrase, "harsh outer walls," Steinbeck not only reinforces the defensive ideas of retreat and refuge, but also suggests another idea—an offensive barrier against outsiders, the barrier of racial prejudice, from behind which the economic, social, and cultural oppression of the community by the town is advanced. But this barrier is callously camouflaged with bougainvillaea. Here too, however, the camouflage itself is descriptive of the town, for the blossoms of the bougainvillaea are symbolic in color: the purple can represent royalty or imperial rank, the *conquistadores* of the Spanish kings whose descendants are the oppressors of Kino's people, or it can symbolize the heinous sins of prejudice and avarice; brick-red can represent the extent of the hatred of the town for the community or, more likely, the blood that has been shed in the subjugation of the Indians; white, although it very often suggests innocence and purity, can also symbolize cowardice or can refer to the white vestments of the clergy, specifically the white cassock or surplice of some of the mendicant orders in early Mexico, and to the royalist, conservative, anti-Indian political viewpoint.

We have finally worked back to the key phrase, "city of stone and plaster," by which Steinbeck combines all that has been suggested about the town with what he will reveal in the nameless individuals of the town. "Stone" continues to represent endurance, strength, refuge, protection, coldness, and harshness; the image created by "plaster," however, is again that of camouflage, the shell-like mask worn by the town to conceal its parasitic reality.

STEINBECK'S USE OF METAPHORS

Even in what might be termed indirect description, Steinbeck has pictures of the parasitic relationship between the community and the town. In the first instance of metaphors from the animal world, Steinbeck reports how an ant, a social animal working for the good of its colony, has been trapped by an ant-lion, living near the ant colony to prey upon it for his individual needs. In the same way the individuals of the town have built "traps" to take advantage of the ignorance of the Indians and to prey upon them for whatever they have of wealth, labor, or services. Next the author cites the example of the hungry dogs and pigs of the town which scavenge the beach searching for dead fish or seabirds, the latter here representing the Indians who live off the sea and who for all general purposes are *dead* because they have no power to resist, while the former represent the greedy townspeople. In a third metaphor Steinbeck describes the fish that live near the oyster beds to feed off the rejected oysters and to nibble at the inner shells. Perhaps this is the most forceful of the metaphors, for the author seems to be saying that the Indians, the rejects of modern society, thrown back after having been despoiled of their wealth by that society, are the prey of the townspeople who live nearby and who scavenge even upon the hopes, dreams, and souls of these people. Finally in the metaphor of the large fish feeding on the small fish, Steinbeck supplies a simple restatement of this parasitic relationship between the town and the community, and perhaps a picture of the inevitability of such a relationship in nature.

In summation, then, let us return to that first pair of descriptive phrases for an inventory of the images therein before relating descriptions to the central theme. "Brush houses" suggests contact with the elements, with nature, with life. If there is a strenuous struggle for existence in the community, there is also exhilaration in the confrontation with nature that such dwellings make possible. In addition the possibility or desire for human contact is evident in the

phrase, which suggests openness and a lack of any perma-
nent barriers. In contrast, "stone and plaster houses" creates
further the images of retreat from the vital contest into a protected passivity, of fear of elemental forces, of impregnable
refuge from the uninvited, of aloof coldness.

In Kino's community all have a sense of responsibility to
one another and a respect for the humanity of each. Coyotito's scream attracts the neighbors' sympathetic attention
as well as curiosity, and the neighbors accompany Kino to
the doctor's when the community makes one of its few in-
cursions into the town. Upon the doctor's refusal to treat the
child, the neighbors will not shame Kino and abandon him
so that he will not have to face them. The discovery of the
pearl brings them again, this time to share the joy and
dreams; yet, they are more concerned for Kino than they are
interested in the pearl. The neighbors again come to Kino
when the doctor appears to inflict temporary illness upon
Coyotito. They also go with Kino when he attempts to sell
the pearl as a necessary sign of friendship; and both before
and after the visit, Juan Tomás emerges from the group to
represent the thinking of the community. During the crisis,
Kino could escape; but he will not commit sacrilege against
the community by taking another's boat. Although the
neighbors demonstrate concern at the fire and grief over the
supposed deaths of Kino and his family, Kino's relationship
with the community has been destroyed because of the murder; and he must leave to protect the community and his
brother ("I am like a leprosy.").

PARASITISM

The town, on the other hand, is like a separate organism,
walled off from the life of the community, yet living only to
drain off that life. With the beggars acting as seers for our
benefit, the parasitic relationship becomes clear in the actions of three people of the town, unnamed as if they were
really impersonal forces, yet singled out for individual roles.
It is through them that one can see all the characteristics
that Steinbeck's description has implied.

"The doctor will not come," say the neighbors; and when
the child is taken to him, the doctor will not treat him. As a
person, he is cold and withdrawn from the life around him;
his only concern is his desire to return to France. He has his
"secret garden," his bedroom, where his life is that of a

wealthy French aristocrat. In his actions, the doctor depicts the harsh barriers of prejudice, from his first remarks in refusing to treat Coyotito ("I am a doctor, not a veterinary.") to his apparently callous experiment with the boy, as if he were some laboratory animal. When the doctor puts on his friendly face, his plaster mask, after the pearl has been found, it is only to gain entree into Kino's hut. He has willingly emerged from behind the harsh barrier to use his knowledge and status to discover the pearl's hiding place and to try to steal it. Steinbeck makes us aware of this camouflage by saying that the doctor's purpose had been discerned by the people, for he "was not good at dissembling."

Another dissembler is the priest, whom the news of the pearl has brought probably for the first time in many months to see what part of the wealth he can get for the Church. When he addresses these "children," he makes the words "sound like a benediction." Yet, in the sermon that he gives annually, he associates himself with the town's oppression and strengthens its parasitic stranglehold upon the community by sanctifying it. Like the doctor, at the news of the pearl, the priest reacts selfishly and emerges from behind the protective wall to raid the sudden new wealth of the community.

It is the pearl buyer, however, who wins the prize for best masquerade—always joking, hand-shaking, calling out greetings, a friend and sympathizer to all, but ferret-eyed, masking all emotion behind a stone-walled face, concentrating the nervous energy inherent in the predatory quest of prey in the ceaselessly excited, always secret movements of a coin trick. In league with the other buyers, he tries to cheat Kino—the attack from behind the wall of economic oppression. Indeed, all the pearl buyers represent that wall, for as agents of a single man they stand together as the harsh barrier of monopoly. Yet, each one, since he appears to be an independent agent, acts as camouflage, as a camouflaging blossom hiding that wall. Realizing their failure to cheat Kino, they later try to rob him. Then, directly or indirectly, after Kino has determined to circumvent that wall of monopoly by selling his pearl elsewhere, they destroy all that Kino has of value, his boat and his home.

In general, the townspeople as presented in the novel suggest the characteristics of parasitism, especially the retreat from strenuous struggle, the passive mode of life. In addition, the pearl buyers, as agents of a single unnamed, never introduced individual, show another characteristic, that of retreat from independent endeavor. Finally, the doctor symbolizes the unmistakable degeneration that results from parasitism.

ANIMALISTIC IMAGERY

Up to this point in the story, we can easily see that Kino's community nurtures human relationships and validates the meaning of existence for its members, whereas the town, as far as the community is concerned and Kino in particular, has consistently sought by its manipulation of men to invalidate the meaning of existence, and it succeeds by forcing Kino to leave the community. From this point the images became animalistic, because the human relationships that gave meaning to Kino's existence as a man have been left behind. The pursuers personify the animosity of the town, which in its greed and as an example to others seeks now to destroy utterly the outsider who has defied it. Their destruction and the consequent salvation of the family, although at the sacrifice of one of its members, re-establish the humanity of and the meaning of existence to Kino and Juana only because they return to the community to begin life again by destroying the pearl.

The Pearl: A Parable of the Human Condition

Richard Astro

Steinbeck writes in *The Pearl* that "humans are never satisfied, that you give them one thing and they want something more." This trait, Steinbeck insists, distinguishes the human species from all others. According to Richard Astro, *The Pearl* is a parable of this human condition, of man's search for happiness. As *The Pearl* opens the impoverished fisherman Kino, in his primitive simplicity, is relatively content with his meager lot. When he finds the Pearl of the World, Kino no longer accepts the burden of lifelong poverty; he begins to dream of a better life. Yet after his aspirations end in tragedy, poorer than before, Kino rejects society's illusory offerings, accepts his niche, and casts to sea his pearl. This paradox, Astro suggests, pointedly illustrates the inherent vanity of human wishes. Astro has published numerous articles on John Steinbeck. He is the author of *John Steinbeck and Edward F. Ricketts: The Shaping of a Novelist,* from which this essay is excerpted.

Among Steinbeck's more adroit examinations of human nature in the context of his growing conviction about the ever-increasing nature of man's pursuit of wealth and power is *The Pearl.* Based upon a story he had heard during his expedition with Ricketts to the Gulf of California about a poor Mexican fisherman who found a fabulous pearl which he thought would guarantee his future happiness, but which almost destroyed him before he threw it back into the sea, Steinbeck worked hard on this fable, rewriting it several times. It was finally published in 1947, but went largely unnoticed, and it was not until six years later that the novelist

Excerpted from Richard Astro, *John Steinbeck and Edward F. Ricketts: The Shaping of a Novelist* (Minneapolis: University of Minnesota Press, 1973), pp. 169–72. Copyright 1973 by the University of Minnesota Press. All rights reserved.

cautiously affirmed that *The Pearl* was finally "gathering some friends."

MAN'S SEARCH FOR HAPPINESS

In contrast with the bawdiness of *Cannery Row*, *The Pearl* is a simple, lyrical tale which Steinbeck called "a black and white story like a parable." It is a parable about the search for happiness and the nature of man's need to choose between the inherently benign natural life and the frantic, self-oriented modern world. At the crux of Steinbeck's theme in *The Pearl*, however, is not only a statement about the choice between simplicity and luxury, but also his conviction that human nature makes it impossible for man to choose what Ricketts called "the region of inward adjustments" (characterized by "friendship, tolerance, dignity, or love") until he has attempted to succeed in "the region of outward possessions." At the end of *The Pearl*, Kino, the poor fisherman, realizes the destructive nature of material wealth and hurls the pearl back into the Sea of Cortez, but Steinbeck simultaneously shows his inability to make this decision until his drive for wealth and status has ended in tragedy and disappointment. For unlike Ricketts, who believed that the simple Indians of the Gulf would disparage the quest for material wealth if untouched by the greed of their northern neighbors, Steinbeck writes in *The Pearl* that "humans are never satisfied, that you give them one thing and they want something more." And he insists, paradoxically, that this "is one of the greatest talents the species has and one that has made it superior to animals that are satisfied with what they have." *The Pearl* is Steinbeck's parable of the human dilemma; it is a study of the agony involved in man's recognition of the vanity of human wishes.

At the beginning of Steinbeck's fable, Kino is a poor but mildly satisfied pearl fisherman. A devoted husband and father, his song is the "Song of the Family," which rises "to an aching chord that caught the throat, saying this is safety, this is warmth, this is the *Whole*." He is a man who, like the contented Indians of the Gulf depicted by Ricketts in his Sea of Cortez journal, enjoys a "deep participation with all things, the gift he had from his people."

> He heard every little sound of the gathering night, the sleepy complaint of settling birds, the love agony of cats, the strike and withdraw of little waves on the beach, and the simple

MEXICO: A TRAVELLER'S PERSPECTIVE

The Pearl *is set in Mexico in the early twentieth century. Familiarity with the social history of Mexico is essential to understanding the plight of Kino and other poor Indian natives in* The Pearl. *The following excerpts appeared in* Mexico as I Saw It, *a book published in 1911 that records the observations of Mrs. Alec Tweedie, who toured Mexico extensively in the early 1900s.*

They [the Indians] cannot read or write, they do not know how to think; all they want is food and shelter, and so their animal existence continues year in, year out. . . .

With the rich folk marriage is the natural sequence [of courtship], and all goes well, or ought to.

With the poor folk it is otherwise. Enquiries have lately been set on foot concerning the morality of village life, and the consequent discoveries are positively appalling. There are pueblos where no wedding has occurred in a generation! . . .

The Cathedral is a handsome edifice. It represents wealth and splendour. The massive balustrades are of solid silver; the candelabra hanging from the ceiling are beautiful, and on this occasion some thousands of candles shed a lurid glow on all around. The priests in gorgeous robes, the decorations of flowers and palms, the quantities of incense giving cloud-like mysticism to the scene, told of wealth unbounded, while kneeling upon the stone flags in various stages of poverty and abject rags were the Indians. Oh, how poor they were!

Claudia Durst Johnson, *Understanding* Of Mice and Men, The Red Pony, *and* The Pearl: *A Student Casebook to Issues, Sources, and Historical Documents,* 1997.

hiss of distance. And he could smell the sharp odor of exposed kelp from the receding tide.

But despite his sense of participation with the land and with his family, Kino is victimized by his poverty and exploited because of his ignorance. "He was trapped as his people were always trapped and would be until . . . they could be sure that the things in the books were really in the books." When, therefore, Kino finds "the pearl of the world," he sees in it an end to the poverty and exploitation which heretofore he has been forced to accept. Gradually, the "Song of the Pearl" merges with the "Song of the Family," Steinbeck points out, "so that the one beautified the other." And Kino envisages a day when he will be able to afford to send his child to school so that "one of his own people could tell him the truth of things." Kino tells his wife, Juana, "This is our one chance. Our son must go to school. He must break out of the pot that holds us in."

But Kino's thinking about the future becomes cloudy; his vision becomes as hazy as the mirage of the Gulf. "There was no certainty in seeing, no proof that what you saw was there or was not there." And Kino looks down into the surface of his fabulous pearl and forms misty, insubstantial dreams that will never come true. For "in this Gulf of uncertain light there were more illusions than realities."

THE TOWN AS AN ORGANISM

As a member of a village of pearl fishermen, Kino is a member-unit in the organism of the greater community of La Paz. Steinbeck describes the town organismically as "a thing like a colonial animal. A town has a nervous system and a head and shoulders and feet. A town is a thing separate from all other towns, so that there are not two towns alike. And a town has a whole emotion." Thus, when Kino finds his great pearl, the organism of the town stirs to life and an interest develops in Kino—"people with things to sell and people with favors to ask."

> The essence of pearl mixed with essence of men and a curious dark residue was precipitated. Every man suddenly became related to Kino's pearl, and Kino's pearl went into the dreams, the speculations, the schemes, the plans, the futures, the wishes, the needs, the lusts, the hungers, of everyone, and only one person stood in the way and that was Kino, so that he became curiously every man's enemy.

No one resented Kino as long as he was an impoverished fisherman. But Kino stirred the fantasies of the townspeople, and upset the equilibrium of the organism.

> If every single man and woman, child and baby, acts and conducts itself in a known pattern and breaks no walls and differs with no one and experiments in no way and is not sick and does not endanger the ease and peace of mind or steady unbroken flow of the town, then that unit can disappear and never be heard of. But let one man step out of the regular thought or the known and trusted pattern, and the nerves of the townspeople ring with nervousness and communication travels over the nerve lines of the town. Then every unit communicates to the whole.

When he senses the greed of the envious villagers, Kino, who "had broken through the horizons into a cold and lonely outside" (Steinbeck's choice of words is significant here), hardens and "his eyes and his voice were hard and cold and a brooding hate was growing in him." And as attempts are made first to cheat him of his wealth and later to steal his pearl, the "Song of the Pearl" becomes a "Song of Evil" as Kino fights to save himself, his family, and his newfound wealth. Kino admits that "This pearl has become my soul. . . . If I give it up I shall lose my soul."

Gradually, Kino realizes that while he has irrevocably lost one world, he has not gained another. He insists that because "I am a man," "I will fight this thing" and "win over it," and he drives "his strength against a mountain" and plunges "against the sea." But Kino's hopes are destroyed, for as Juana, his ostensibly suppliant but strong and knowing wife (like Ma Joad, Juana is "pure Briffault"), realizes, "the mountain would stand while the man broke himself"; "the sea would surge while the man drowned in it." At the same time, Juana knows that it is the striving that makes Kino a man, "half insane and half god, and Juana had need of a man."

Choosing the Simple Life

Kino saves his pearl from those who would steal it, but he pays dearly for it with the destruction of his house and canoe, and ultimately with the death of his baby. Finally, Kino begins to see the pearl as a "grey, malignant growth," and he chooses the "region of inward adjustments" over the "region of outward possessions" by throwing the pearl back into the Gulf. And though he has lost his canoe, his home, and his child, and so is even poorer than before, his choice has been made possible only because he has "gone through the pain" and "come out on the other side." Kino's story is the parable of the human condition; a parable of that two-legged paradox, man, growing accustomed to "the tragic miracle of consciousness," struggling, and finally succeeding, to forge the design of his microcosmic history.

While Ricketts' ideas about the inherent virtues of the simple, natural life serve as a thematic substratum on which Steinbeck builds his parable, the novelist's chief concern in *The Pearl* is with how man's failure to "participate" in "the region of inward adjustments" can lead to complete personal and social disintegration.

CHAPTER 2

Symbols, Language, and Structural Devices

The Allegory of *The Pearl*

Peter Lisca

Steinbeck scholar Peter Lisca describes *The Pearl* as
too long and too complex to be a parable, which illustrates a single moral or principle; rather, he la-
bels it an allegory, specifically an "allegory of the
soul," of what distinguishes human consciousness
and potential from the rest of nature. On this level of
allegory, Lisca analyzes how Steinbeck incorporates
particular myths, such as Eden references and mythical elements from Indian cultures, to reinforce the
story's rich layers of meaning. Lisca is a professor of
English at the University of Florida. He is the author
of numerous articles and several books critiquing
Steinbeck's works, including *John Steinbeck: Nature
and Myth*, from which the following critical essay is
excerpted.

Although Steinbeck was correct in calling his first 200-word
version of his story a "parable," that term is not quite accurate for *The Pearl*. Not only is it too long for a parable, but too
complex and rich in meaning. "Allegory" is a better term, especially if we have in mind its rich medieval forms, for this
novelette exists on a number of levels. It is also an allegory
of the soul. The title itself indicates several possible sources.
First to come to mind is Matthew 13:45, 46, Jesus' parable of
the "pearl of great price." But, as we have seen before, Steinbeck's reading led him much further afield than his Bible.
There is also the anonymous medieval poem, *Pearl*, and,
somewhat more recondite, the gnostic fragment called "Acts
of Thomas," which contains one passage sometimes printed
separately as "The Song of the Pearl." In all three of these
sources the pearl is read as a symbol for the soul, and the allegory is understood to treat of its redemption. In fact, the

Excerpted from *John Steinbeck: Nature and Myth*, by Peter Lisca. Copyright © 1978 by
Peter Lisca. Reprinted by permission of HarperCollins Publishers, Inc.

gnostic passage is called also "The Hymn of the Soul." There
are suggestions that Steinbeck had all three sources in mind.
From the medieval poem Steinbeck may have taken the idea
for the music images and, most important, the father-child-
pearl association. In the "Acts of Thomas" he could have
found the idea of the soul's being in bondage and the perilous quest of redeeming it. However, Steinbeck's allegory of
the pearl-soul goes far beyond all of these sources.

ALLEGORY OF THE SOUL

Although almost all the action is Kino's and it is he who says
several times, "This pearl has become my soul," and "If I
give it up I shall lose my soul," nevertheless it is *his* soul in
an interestingly indirect manner. Kino finds the pearl after
Juana has prayed that he may find a pearl to pay a doctor to
cure their little son of a scorpion sting. There is never any
question but that the pearl is for the child, even after the doctor is not needed. In the boat, while Kino is hesitating to
open the unusual oyster, Juana "put her hand on Coyotito's
covered head. 'Open it,' she said softly." When the oyster is
opened and the pearl disclosed, immediately, for no apparent reason, "Instinctively Juana went to Coyotito where he
lay in his father's blanket. She lifted the poultice of seaweed
and looked . . . the swelling was going out of the baby's
shoulder, the poison was receding from its body." Later,
when Juana steals the pearl from Kino's hiding place to
throw it away, fearful of the danger it has brought, she
pauses first at Coyotito's crib. Near the end of the book,
when Kino urges his wife to keep Coyotito quiet so that he
may surprise and kill their pursuers, who would take away
the pearl, Juana replies, "He will not cry. . . . He knows." Fur-
thermore, the very name Coyotito ("little coyote") signifies
the animal nature of a creature which does not have a soul;
his crying is once described as like "a coyote pup."

The redeeming of the pearl, then, is equivalent to raising
this being from an animal to a human state. For clearly the
pearl symbolizes not the usual religious definition of "soul,"
but human consciousness and potential, those qualities that
cause man to separate himself from the rest of Nature. This
is signified by the education which the pearl will buy, to literally raise Coyotito from the almost animal existence into
which he was born. Kino's identification of the pearl with
his own soul is by two extensions. First, Coyotito is his son—

himself a child again, an extension of himself into the future. Secondly, Coyotito's education (what the pearl will buy and thus its equivalent), or soul, "will make us free . . . he will know and through him we will know." In this extension, the allegory of the soul now applies not only to Kino but to the entire Indian community. Consider also that Kino, as the priest reminds him, is named after the Jesuit missionary Father Eusebius Kino, a great saver of souls among the Indians of that region.

DARK FORCES

In any allegory about the soul, there are evil powers that attempt to thwart its redemption. In Steinbeck's novelette these are conspicuously mysterious, referred to as "the dark unhuman things," "watchful evil," "dark creeping things,"

THE PEARL: A COMPLEX WORK

Since The Pearl*'s publication, many readers have called the novel an allegory. In the following excerpt, however, Steinbeck scholar John H. Timmerman describes why he believes that the novel does not fit the parameters of true allegory.*

The Pearl, while often and offhandedly referred to as an allegory (as is *The Wayward Bus*), is in fact not one. All great literature suggests meanings that lie beyond the immediate narrative level, but very few do so in a strictly allegorical fashion marked by the intensity and consistency of two separate levels of meaning—narrative and allegorical. In allegory the author deliberately patterns the fictional world to suggest specific meanings to the reader, and the author must pattern the work with hard rigidity. To be successful, the allegorical work must be self-restrictive; that is to say, a figure who on page one represents death may not on page ten represent life. Moving without variation from the plane of the narrative to the plane of the predetermined allegorical meaning, the story is essentially two-dimensional. In fact, any lessening or wavering in the two-dimensional unity, or any admission of more than one theme, lessens the worth of the work as allegory. The task of the reader upon considering allegory is to establish that two-dimensional interplay in his own mind. The matter is one of puzzle solving, of arranging the pieces within their narrative frame; and it is a matter of solving someone else's puzzle, not making and solving one's own.

John H. Timmerman, *John Steinbeck's Fiction: The Aesthetics of the Road Taken,* 1986.

"shadowy and dreadful," "the dark ones," and the like. They are the ones who three times attack Kino to rob him of the pearl. The two trackers and the horseman, also, who pursue Kino and his family are made symbolically suggestive. But again on this level of the allegory, the moral is in the ending. For neither is Kino defeated by these evil powers, nor does he redeem his pearl. Instead, he chooses to renounce it after overcoming the powers of darkness. Kino refuses the option of attaining his soul (a distinct identity) at such continued cost, preferring to *undefine* himself, returning the seed of individual soul to [Walt] Whitman's cosmic "Float," [Ralph Waldo] Emerson's (and Casy's) Oversoul, thus going back to the blameless bosom of Nature in a quasi-animal existence— "in the near dark" of the story's opening sentence.

It is also possible to see in *The Pearl* still another of Steinbeck's several Eden myths, with a unique twist. After eating of the forbidden tree ("Yes, God punished Kino because he rebelled against the way things are"), after being expelled from the Garden ("We must go away"), and after experiencing the land that lies "east of Eden" (the rock and desert landscape of their flight), Kino and Juana return to Eden, put the apple back on the tree, as it were. They reject the "fortunate fall" which would give man the burden of an immortal soul to save or damn, and return to an animal-like life, Adam and Eve before the Fall. All these readings are suggested within the structure and rich texture of *The Pearl.*

INDIAN MYTHOLOGY

The allegory extends also into Mexican Indian mythology. Although Steinbeck always presents Kino and Juana as basically Indian in consciousness, he carefully leaves their particular origins vague, because the peoples of Baja California seem to have been much weaker in religious ritualism than those of the mainland and almost nothing is known of the ancient religion of the Seri Indians of the La Paz area except that they existed on an animistic level which attributed life and supernatural powers to all things. (Coyotito, however, is named after one of the four Seri clans—Coyote.) Therefore, Steinbeck uses mythical elements from various Indian cultures, but especially the Mayan and the Aztec, which are dominant in our general knowledge of pre-Columbian Mexico. This material is so rich, and Steinbeck's utilization of it so detailed that it bulks larger than the Christian elements in the novelette as well as in the consciousness of Kino and Juana themselves.

To begin with, in stressing so often the novelette's imprecise landscape, its "mist," its "hazy mirage . . . the uncertain air . . . so that all sights were unreal and vision could not be trusted," Steinbeck suggests not only the generally dreamlike settings of fabular literature, but quite specifically a Mayan belief that in the most recent creation the gods saw that they had made man too gifted and therefore had to place a mist before his eyes so that the secrets of the universe would not be revealed to him. Another general and significant aspect is the novelette's time span. In the incredibly accurate Mayan calendar, at the end of one of the major cycles (fifty-two years), and before the beginning of the next, there were the *Uayeb,* "five unlucky days" of great significance, including ritualistic destruction of furniture, bloodletting, lamentation and extinguishing of all fires—at the end of which a new fire was kindled and a new cycle began. During these five days, possible catastrophe was imminent, and it was best to stay at home. It can hardly be coincidental that from the morning of the day on which Kino wakens at the beginning of the novel, and during which he finds the pearl, to sunset on the evening of the story's ending, when Kino and Juana return from their journey and throw the pearl back into the sea, the time span is exactly five days, at the end of which destruction and suffering, man and wife resume their usual cycle.

LIGHT AND DARKNESS

Another large symbolic element is the novelette's constant and suggestive use of light and darkness. Generally among these Indians (as other peoples) darkness is feared because it is then that evil forces and the creatures of darkness are free to bring about man's destruction. In *The Pearl* this association is suggested throughout and often insisted upon: "and with the darkness came the music of evil again," "his fear of dark and the devils that haunt the night." The Indians cover their faces against the darkness; the three assaults upon Kino are in the night and, as discussed above, the assailants linked with the world of darkness. In various ways, even the doctor, the priest (both of whom visit Kino at night), and the pearl buyers are linked to darkness. Thus the scene in which Kino begins to fear the light and associate himself with the darkness, after killing one assailant and finding his house on fire, is significant. His flight begins in darkness; he attacks his three pursuers at night; and it is then that his son is killed. The owl, one of the Mayan symbols of evil and death, is conspicuous in the night scenes.

Inevitably associated with night is the moon, in Mayan mythology one of the two important sky gods, inconstant and malicious in character. In the novelette the moon reappears from behind the clouds to show Juana the pearl after Kino loses it; as the clouds again cover the moon, she thinks of completing her intention of throwing the pearl into the sea, but the moon again reappears and shows her the two men lying in the path ahead of her, one of whom is Kino, whom she runs to help. The moon also reappears, rising sooner than expected, as Kino is preparing to leap upon his pursuers, causing the delay (and perhaps Coyotito's cry) which allows the fatal shot. The pearl itself is described "perfect as the moon," is seen to glitter in moonlight, and reflects the moon in its surface, thus reinforcing frequent suggestions that the pearl is evil. As in Mayan mythology the sun is the other important sky god, associated with the powers of life and goodness and antagonist to the moon, so in the novelette daylight dispels the powers of darkness, a process that is generally suggested in *The Pearl* by Steinbeck's descriptions of the dawn. In reference to this struggle and the pearl's association with the moon, it is relevant that Kino's name has its origin not only in the Jesuit missionary, but in the Mayan word *Kin*, meaning sun. The clouds which try to hide the moon in the above passages come from the south, domain of the sun. Of the several visions that Kino sees in the pearl's surface, all are delusions except one, the last, the only one seen in the open light of day, just before he flings it back into the sea: "He looked into its surface and it was gray and ulcerous. Evil faces peered from it into his eyes, and he saw the light of burning. . . . The pearl was ugly; it was gray like a malignant growth . . . the music of the pearl distorted and insane."

Steinbeck's reading in Mexican sources was extensive, and mythology had always a particular interest for him. He chose his Indian materials carefully to reinforce his other levels of meaning. In this novelette of eighty pages Steinbeck attains what is very difficult and rare in even the best allegories—a congruence of all its referential levels. *The Pearl* achieves a dimension beyond that possible to realistic fiction.

Symbols and Imagery in *The Pearl*

John H. Timmerman

According to John H. Timmerman, Steinbeck infuses *The Pearl* with symbols and imagery to create patterns that guide interpretation of the story. Specifically, Timmerman notes the pattern created by the interplay of light and dark imagery, as when physical darkening mirrors Kino's fear and anxiety. Animal imagery, too, is highly functional, becoming increasingly predatory as Kino's troubles deepen. Finally, the Song of the Family and the Song of Evil provide not only a structural device for the story, but also assume symbolic significance as the tension between the two escalates. John H. Timmerman is the author of *John Steinbeck's Fiction: The Aesthetics of the Road Taken*, from which this critical essay is excerpted.

Although [critic] Harry Morris was correct in his judgment that "John Steinbeck has never been very far away from the allegorical method. Some of his earliest work—and among that, his best—shows involvement with elements of allegory," one should not confuse involvement with allegory as the allegorical method itself. Steinbeck's involvement with allegory operates on the level of a rich suggestiveness in story, but with characters and thematic plot development coming first. Story, for Steinbeck, is never a handmaiden to meaning; rather the meanings that arise are constructed in suggestive analogues or symbols in the work, which may open different doors of signification for any individual reader, so that the reader apprehends spiritual patterns or abstractions that have been stimulated by certain literary figures, symbols, or devices. By repetition of pointing signals, or symbols, the author constructs a pattern that guides the interpretation. . . .

Excerpted from *John Steinbeck's Fiction: The Aesthetics of the Road Taken*, by John H. Timmerman. Copyright © 1986 by the University of Oklahoma Press, Norman, Publishing Division of the University. Reprinted with permission of the publisher.

The essential outline of plot and theme is charged with symbolism and suggestiveness. The symbols in the story are not abrupt, sudden, or confusing; rather they emerge naturally and powerfully from a carefully arranged symbolic environment cast in the narrative framework. In its broadest pattern the novella is a kind of reversal of the biblical Book of Job: the story of a man who has everything, then loses everything, finally to gain back "twice as much as he had before" (Job 42:10). Kino is the man who has nothing, gains the pearl of the world, and ends with less than he began with, save for the knowledge that he now knows and has experienced the lie of civilization's lures.

PATTERNED IMAGERY

More specifically, however, the work is framed by several kinds of patterned imagery, primary among which is that referring to light. The novella begins in "near dark" that washes into golden morning, "a morning like other mornings and yet perfect among mornings." The crystal clarity is shattered when Coyotito is stung by the scorpion, and the following morning dawns in a haze: "Although the morning was young, the hazy mirage was up. The uncertain air that magnified some things and blotted out others hung over the whole Gulf so that all lights were unreal and vision could not be trusted; so that sea and land had the sharp clarities and vagueness of a dream." And through this haze, appropriately, we catch a glimpse of the region of the town: "Across the estuary from the town one section of mangroves stood clear and telescopically defined, while another mangrove clump was a hazy black-green blob. Part of the far shore disappeared into a shimmer that looked like water. There was no certainty in seeing." By the time the villagers journey into the town itself, the light has faded, to be replaced by an oppressive blackness symbolic of the villagers' greed: "The news stirred up something infinitely black and evil in the town; the black distillate was like the scorpion."

FROM LIGHTNESS TO DARKNESS

By chapter 5, after the open conflict in the town, the atmosphere has become opaque and dim. This time Kino "opened his eyes in the darkness." Only the pale light of the moon stabs the gloom. The shift from brightness to darkness and from clarity to obscurity is accompanied by a decisive shift in color emphasis, from the clear golds, yellows, and earth hues of green and brown that dominate the first chapter to more emotionally charged colors. In chapter 5, Kino's "brain was red with anger." Now the light that was formerly a source of joy becomes a threat: "Suddenly Kino was afraid. The light made him afraid. He remembered the man lying dead in the brush beside the path, and he took Juana by the arm and drew her into the shadow of a house away from the light, for light was danger to him." And the physical darkening in the novella is mirrored psychologically in Kino's own fear and uncertainty:

> In a few moments Juan Tomás came back with her. He lighted a candle and came to them where they crouched in a corner and he said, "Apolonia, see to the door, and do not let anyone enter." He was older, Juan Tomás, and he assumed the authority. "Now, my brother," he said.
> "I was attacked in the dark," said Kino. "And in the fight I have killed a man."
> "Who?" asked Juan Tomás quickly.
> "I do not know. It is all darkness—all darkness and the shape of darkness."

Such characters fumble in a morass of darkness. Kino, Juana, and Coyotito climb into the tenebrous and threatening mountains from which "the sun had passed." They head west, into the dying sunlight, and wander a maze of crooked chasms. Finally, it is "late in the golden afternoon" when Kino and Juana attempt to reclaim the light by hurling the pearl into the sea. As they walk toward the sea, "The sun was behind them and their long shadows stalked ahead, and they seemed to carry two towers of darkness with them." Only when the pearl disappears beneath the waves do we get a suggestion of renewed light:

> And the pearl settled into the lovely green water and dropped toward the bottom. The waving branches of the algae called to it and beckoned to it. The lights on its surface were green and lovely. It settled down to the sand bottom among the fernlike plants. Above, the surface of the water was a green mirror.

ANIMAL IMAGERY

The transition in light imagery from gentle familiarity to the fearsome dark is paralleled in the book through increasingly predatory animal imagery. The setting at large is carefully established in animal imagery—the colonial organism, the devouring power of civilization, the doctor's regard for the

FOLKLORE IN *THE PEARL*
In a review of The Pearl *written shortly after its publication, critic Carlos Baker finds the tale anchored in a rich
bounty of folklore.*

In turning from the background of [*The Pearl*] to what the
Middle Ages would have called its "mystery," one is chiefly
struck by the number of points at which the tale impinges,
through Steinbeck's artfully simple rendering of it, on the un-
killable folklore of Palestine, Greece, Rome, China, India and
the whole sweep of western Europe from the Scandinavian to
the Iberian peninsula. For the pearl which the Mexican fisherman Kino dug from the Gulf of California was concealed in
the center of the golden fruit of the Hesperides, and its seeds
were at the core of another apple in a fair Mesopotamian garden called Eden. Its death-dealing luster glinted in certain
fabulous gold coins in the hands of beggars in ancient Bagh-
dad; King Midas knew its power and felt its pain. It was
guarded by fire-spewing dragons in the lonely stone cairns of
the Norsemen; certain German princes found its prototype in
the treasure boxes of bewhiskered cannibalistic giants; and
one heard of something like it in the smoky longhouses of the
Algonquin Indians. In a hundred metamorphoses it nestled
among the foliage on [Sir James George] Frazer's *Golden
Bough*. One of its names is the power of good and evil.

Carlos Baker, *New York Times Book Review*, November 30, 1947.

Indians as so many insects—but the progress of the pearl's
influence on Kino is also measured by his devolution into
the animalistic. His very finding of the pearl, in fact, announces the transformation: "Kino's fist closed over the
pearl and his emotion broke over him. He put his head back
and howled. His eyes rolled up and he screamed and his
body was rigid." From that point on, the animal imagery
steadily becomes more grim and feral, as a primitive hatred
rises in Kino.

It is impossible to list all the examples of animal imagery
in the book, but the following illustrate the transformation of
Kino revealed in animal imagery. When he goes to sell the
pearl, "Kino had grown tight and hard. He felt the creeping
of fate, the circling of wolves, the hover of vultures." When
Juana attempts to throw the pearl away, "Kino looked down
at her and his teeth were bared. He hissed at her like a
snake, and Juana stared at him with wide unfrightened eyes,

like a sheep before the butcher." When attacked by robbers, "Kino moved sluggishly, arms and legs stirred like those of a crushed bug, and a thick muttering came from his mouth." When his canoe is destroyed, "He was an animal now, for hiding, for attacking, and he lived only to preserve himself and his family." When he flees the village, "Some ancient thing stirred in Kino. Through his fear of dark and the devils that haunt the night, there came a rush of exhilaration; some animal thing was moving in him so that he was cautious and wary and dangerous; some ancient thing out of the past of his people was alive in him." And finally, when pursued, "Kino edged like a slow lizard down the smooth rock shoulder," and "The Song of the Family had become as fierce and sharp and feline as the snarl of a female puma." The steps trace the reversion in Kino to the primitive and predatory. Touched by the malignancy of civilization, he has become one of the "tigers" of Cannery Row.

THE SONG OF THE FAMILY

Operating concomitantly with the darkening light imagery, intensifying color imagery, and increasingly predatory animal imagery that mark Kino's dark night of the soul, is the transformation in the quasi-symbolic Song of the Family. This fascinating structural device forms a part of the realistic narrative level as an actual song of the Indian families but assumes symbolic significance as the novella progresses. Thus it operates at two levels—structural technique and symbol—and forms a transition to the larger symbolism of the story.

As part of the native reality recounted in the narrative plot, the Song of the Family is of a piece with the religious fabric woven into the daily lives of the Indians, a fabric curiously steeped in Christianity and folk tradition: "The scorpion moved delicately down the rope toward the box. Under her breath Juana repeated an ancient magic to guard against such evil, and on top of that she muttered a Hail Mary between clenched teeth." The Song of the Family is part of the daily structure, a melody of life in order, and a life in harmony with God. But the song quickly assumes symbolic significance as the tension between the Song of the Family and the Song of Evil intensifies.

The song established early in the story speaks to the order of daily life, the history and unity of the people, and all the small things that make life commonplace and good. This virtue of the commonplace, this natural rhythm of life, are what greed and civilization destroy; and once destroyed they are impossible to recover. There is no going back, no going home again. But for a time the people live in the midst of the measured harmony that emanates from nature and the people themselves:

> Kino heard the little splash of morning waves on the beach. It was very good—Kino closed his eyes again to listen to his music. Perhaps he alone did this, and perhaps all of his people did it. His people had once been great makers of songs so that everything they saw or thought or did or heard became a song. That was very long ago. The songs remained; Kino knew them, but no new songs were added. That does not mean that there were no personal songs. In Kino's head there was a song now, clear and soft, and if he had been able to speak of it, he would have called it the Song of the Family.

While the making of songs roots the people in a tradition, each small task of daily life participates in an ongoing rhythm and melody. While Juana was grinding corn, "the rhythm of the family song was the grinding stone where Juana worked the corn for the morning cakes." While she was rocking Coyotito, she "sang softly an ancient song that had only three notes and yet endless variety of interval. And this was part of the family song too. It was all part. Sometimes it rose to an aching chord that caught the throat, saying this is safety, this is warmth, this is the *Whole*."

The song begins to change with the first minute movements of the scorpion on the crib ropes: "In his mind a new song had come, the Song of Evil, the music of the enemy, of any foe of the family, a savage, secret, dangerous melody, and underneath, the Song of the Family cried plaintively." The scorpion is prefigurative of the internal "sting of evil" that the pearl poses. One is outward and physical, the other inward and spiritual. Each is equally malevolent and heralded by the Song of Evil before which the Song of the Family quails.

THE MUSIC OF THE PEARL

Into this dialectic of the family song and the evil song, one symbolizing order and harmony, the other disorder and destruction, enters the Music of the Pearl. There is a curious neutrality of the theme here. The pearl song in and of itself is not evil; it is merely music. How people play the music, one might say, constitutes the good or evil. The Music of the Pearl is first introduced as possibility, a "counter-melody" within the Song of the Family, a part of its harmony yet somehow counter to it: "But in the song there was a secret little inner song, hardly perceptible, but always there, sweet and secret and clinging, almost hiding in the counter-melody, and this was the Song of the Pearl That Might Be." In fact, once the pearl is found, the Song of the Family runs apace in its natural rhythm; the Music of the Pearl even seems to strengthen and solidify the family song: "And the music of the pearl had merged with the music of the family so that one beautified the other."

But possibility is always attended by ambiguity. For Kino the pearl opens the door on the possibility of owning the power tools of civilization. For the doctor, the merchants, and others, it opens on greed. As Kino's own dreams are consumed by greed, the Song of the Family grows uncertain and disturbed: "Now uncertainty was in Kino, and the music of evil throbbed in his head and nearly drove out Juana's song." And the music, with uncertainty, changes dramatically to a dark, pulsing beat of evil.

With the attempt to sell the pearl and the open exposure of human greed, the Song of Evil rises and drowns out that of the family. Juana notes this most perceptively and struggles to retain the natural rhythms:

> Juana watched him with worry, but she knew him and she knew she could help him best by being silent and by being near. And as though she too could hear the song of Evil, she fought it, singing softly the melody of the family, of the safety and warmth and wholeness of the family. She held Coyotito in her arms and sang the song to him, to keep the evil out, and her voice was brave against the threat of the dark music.

In her effort to preserve the natural harmony and to secure the Song of the Family, Juana tries to throw the pearl away. This in itself exposes a terrible breach in the family, for it pits one member of the family against another. But from the start Juana has recognized the terror represented by the pearl and its dark, threatening music: "'This thing is evil,' she cries harshly. 'This pearl is like a sin! It will destroy us,' and her voice rose shrilly." Not until the end does Kino recognize her wisdom, which he sanctions by handing her the pearl to throw away. In this crucial scene Kino acknowledges Juana as the victor over evil and her essential rightness in spiritual perception. Until that time the Song of Evil rises to a shrill, howling pitch. All melody and harmony seem lost: "Now the darkness was closing in on his family; now the evil music filled the night, hung over the mangroves, skirled in the wave beat." Finally, in this battle of songs the Song of the Family must itself become fierce and predatory, something eminently dear and worth battling for. When Kino and Juana battle the trackers in the mountains, the Song of the Family rises like the fierce cry of the female puma, and as they walk back through the town, "in Kino's ears the Song of the Family was as fierce as a cry."

The final sentence in the book notes the dissipation of threat: "The music of the pearl drifted to a whisper and disappeared." One assumes that order has been restored, and in a way it has been. Even though the price has been paid, the pearl tossed into the sea, and the priceless pearl of Coyotito offered like a propitiation to human greed, the Song of the Family has emerged stronger, victorious.

THE SYMBOLIC SIGNIFICANCE OF THE PEARL

This major thematic pattern of the dialectic of songs is sustained by degrees of symbolic significance in the story, chief of which is the pearl itself. Although like its music the pearl is simply an object and therefore neutral, achieving symbolic significance in how it is used, the pearl has the possibility of transforming the human spirit. The obvious symbolism, of course, is that the pearl represents Kino's dreams of social aspiration and achievement. In chapter 3 at each stage of his dreaming of things that the pearl will make possible, he sees the fulfillment of the dream mirrored in the pearl. For example, the final dream is for Coyotito's education, which will ensure social position: "In the pearl Kino saw himself and Juana squatting by the little fire in the brush hut while Coyotito read from a great book." Thus the pearl represents a dream and a hope for the future, but the dream turns nightmare. One often observes this theme in Steinbeck's earlier work, always with the effect that dreams will be dashed against the monolithic shores of civilization's greed.

On a second level of meaning the pearl reflects the mutations of Kino's own soul. After his dreaming, Kino closed his fist on the pearl "and cut the light away from it." At the same time he closed the light on his own soul, a fact that he openly confesses as he flees the village: "'This pearl has become my soul,' said Kino. 'If I give it up I shall lose my soul.'" It is true that the pearl is by now an inward thing, the physical object simply a symbol of the spiritual struggle between the Song of the Family and the Song of Evil at war within Kino. Only when the Song of the Family begins to emerge victoriously in the mountains can Kino see the hideousness of greed, a third level of meaning represented in the pearl: "He looked into its surface and it was gray and ulcerous. Evil faces peered from it into his eyes and he saw the light of burning." Finally, the pearl represents liberation for Kino, at first from the old family structures as he dreams of his wealth, but ultimately and ironically from the lures of civilization and wealth themselves as he is liberated to throw away the pearl and to return to the Song of the Family.

MINOR SYMBOLS

Other minor symbols work quietly in the novella. The Indian boats represent to the people a heritage and tradition, a way of life and a part of the Song of the Family. Such is also the case with Kino's canoe, inherited from his father and emblematic of long tradition:

> Kino and Juana came slowly to down to the beach and to Kino's canoe, which was the one thing of value he owned in the world. It was very old, Kino's grandfather had brought it from Nayarit, and he had given it to Kino's father, and so it had come to Kino. It was at once property and source of food, for a man with a boat can guarantee a woman that she will eat something. It is the bulwark against starvation. And every year Kino refinished his canoe with the hard shell-like plaster by the secret method that had also come to him from his father.

The destruction of the canoe thus represents a destruction of one's most sacred treasure, as if the altar of a temple were defiled and something beyond price, beyond even the pearl of the world, were lost: "The canoe of his grandfather, plastered over and over, and a splintered hole broken in it. This was an evil beyond thinking. The killing of a man was not so evil as the killing of a boat."

Another minor symbol is the rifle, which appears in the story twice, first in Kino's dream of a Winchester in which it represents an unattainable dream of power, freedom, and wealth, and then as the actual rifle used during the manhunt, in which it represents only death, terror, and fear. It is significant that Kino returns to the shore carrying the rifle; the Song of the Family will be protected by its power, but also the only dream Kino has realized from his early list is the rifle with its death-bringing power.

Finally, as in so many of his other novels, one should include the mountains as symbolic of the escalating series of obstacles, and the hard, mounting urgency of confrontation in the novel. As with Pepe in the short story "Flight," the mountains also represent self-discovery and ultimately death.

One might charge that Steinbeck has written a story only to sustain a pattern of symbolism. But there is a kind of deft artistic simplicity in the novella that counters the charge. Technically this derives from a narrative objectivity with, save for the prefatory note, little authorial intrusion. There is very little dialogue in the tale, with concentration chiefly upon Kino's character as it is presented in a documentary fashion. The action is direct, and the plot is perfectly developed. In sum, *The Pearl* is a simple, unpretentious, and successful work in which Steinbeck seems to have worked out and settled his theme of nearly two decades, pitting the individual and his dreams against the threat of social power structures.

Language Devices in *The Pearl*

John M. Nagle

While many Steinbeck critics focus their analysis on character, plot, and theme, John M. Nagle believes that to truly appreciate Steinbeck's skill as a writer, a reader must also understand how Steinbeck purposefully shapes his language to infuse meaning into his prose. In the following essay Nagle analyzes specific language devices—word choice, word order, and sentence structure—employed by Steinbeck in *The Pearl*. Nagle was a professor of English at the University of Pittsburgh when he contributed this article to the *English Journal*.

The truly sensitive and creative writer shapes his language. In a way which is characteristically his, he manipulates the words and syntactic structures common to us all so that his resulting language does more than simply *express* his intended meaning—it deliberately *intensifies* or *reinforces* the essence of that meaning. The writer is therefore concerned not only with *what* he says, but to an even greater extent with *how* he says it. To be successful in this manipulation of language, he is always alert to the consequences of word choice and word order, the various effects of sentence structure and paragraph division, and the rhythm and sound of what he writes. If successful, he has forced language to work for him rather than allowed it to work against him, and his newly-created language has enhanced rather than dissipated the significance of his intended meaning. . . .

Devices of language fall into two general categories: word choice and sentence structure. Word choice includes a writer's deliberate selection of descriptive words (adjectives and adverbs), active and passive verbs, the slang and colloquialisms of dialects, metaphor and simile, verbals, repeti-

Excerpted from John M. Nagle, "A View of Literature Too Often Neglected," *English Journal*, vol. 58, no. 3 (March 1969). Copyright 1969 by the National Council of Teachers of English. Reprinted with permission.

tion, words which personify and animate, and groups of words with alliterative or onomatopoetic value. Sentence structure includes a writer's intelligent use when building sentences of simple and complex structures, straight-ahead and inverted structures, fragments and run-ons, repetition of structures, slot-slipping, active and passive construction, rhythm and sound, and punctuation to emphasize or relate ideas. Though this list includes most of the common devices an author may employ, it is by no means complete, nor will the discussion that follows attempt to illustrate all of the possible devices. . . .

John Steinbeck's short novel *The Pearl* lends itself nicely to . . . general analysis of the purposeful use of language devices. . . . Steinbeck . . . relies heavily upon intelligent word choice and deliberate sentence structure as he tells his simple, but beautiful tale of a Mexican Indian and his "pearl of the world."

For Kino and his people, their success as pearl-divers is their chief means of survival. They live a primitive, tribe-like existence, hold to a mixture of superstitious and Christian beliefs, and consider a man's boat to be the "one thing of value" that he owns in the world. They are ignorant of all outside their own tribe and so are an oppressed people, pressured by the priest, tricked by the doctor, and cheated by the pearl-buyers. And yet, as Kino's brother Juan Tomás comments, they are helpless to do anything, for they fear that to break from their primitive existence is to defy "the whole structure, the whole way of life." As a result, Kino and his people are indeed involved in the battle for survival, and their only defense in this battle is to rely upon their primitive instincts. More often than not, their resulting actions and reactions are more those of animals than those of human beings.

KINO AND THE ANIMAL WORLD

If their animal-like actions are to be credible, Steinbeck must early in the novel present the primitive and almost animal-like existence of his main characters, Kino and Juana. If Kino is to be hunted, trapped, and physically defeated like an animal by the novel's end, then Steinbeck must bring out Kino's animal characteristics throughout the entire novel. And he gets off to a good start in the first paragraph of the first chapter. His first sentence, "Kino awakened in the near dark," not only immediately names his main character, but specifies the time when Kino begins his day. As we read on, we become sensitive to the significance of this time, for after his terse introductory sentence—the shortest of the paragraph— Steinbeck shifts his focus away from Kino and to the awakening animal world around Kino. He describes the roosters, pigs, and birds which are also just awakening in the near dark and beginning their own daily battle for survival. Implied throughout the paragraph is a definite parallel between Kino and the animal world around him, and only after Steinbeck has established this important relationship does he return his focus to Kino and develop his narrative.

To emphasize this relationship throughout the novel, Steinbeck manipulates his language and seems to go out of his way to describe the impulsive actions of Kino as very close to those of any animal. Sometimes the relationship is implied, sometimes it is stated, but whether stated or implied it is always there because of Steinbeck's deliberate choice of words. Any number of examples from the novel will illustrate. As he "glided" across the room to kill the scorpion that had struck Coyotito, Kino was "snarling" and "his teeth were bared." As he defended himself from the first attacker who sought his pearl, Kino "sprang like an angry cat, leaped striking and spitting for the dark thing" that he knew instinctively was his enemy. When Juana attempted to throw away the pearl, Kino tracked her to the sea and caught her arm just as she was about to throw the pearl. Kino's rage, totally uncontrolled and completely irrational, drove him to hit and kick his wife and leave her half-conscious among the boulders at the water's edge. And as he was driven by instinct and anger to beat her for attempting to throw the pearl away, Kino's "teeth were bared" and "he hissed at her like a snake." Finally, in the last third of the novel, Steinbeck states the comparison he has been developing. After Kino had killed another attacker and had discovered a great hole in the bottom of his canoe, Steinbeck writes that Kino "was an animal now, for hiding, for attacking, and he lived only to preserve himself and his family." As Kino and his family were escaping from La Paz, "some animal thing was moving in him so that he was cautious and wary and dangerous," and later, with "an animal light in his eyes," he watched the approach of the trackers, and "his lips snarled" as he realized his fate. Instinctively, Kino hastened to the protection of the mountains, and Steinbeck climaxes his basic metaphor with the remark that "Kino ran for the high place, as nearly all animals do when they are pursued."

DELIBERATE WORD CHOICE

To strengthen further the animal-like actions and reactions of Kino, Steinbeck again through his choice of words, attributes similar animal-like qualities both to the other characters in the novel and to the forces which acted upon Kino. On one occasion, Juana's "lips drew back from her teeth like a cat's lips," and as she was severely beaten by her husband, she "stared at him with wide unfrightened eyes, like a sheep before the butcher." The trackers who pursued Kino and his family into the mountains were as "sensitive as hounds" and they "scuttled over the ground like animals" and "whined a little, like excited dogs on a warming trail." And even the town of La Paz becomes animated and takes on the sharp characteristics of "a colonial animal." It has "a nervous system and a head and shoulders and feet." It has an emotion and is able to keep track "of itself and of all its units." And it has "poison sacs" which manufacture the venom of greed and cause it to swell and puff. Perhaps Steinbeck's most attention-calling word choice is his description of the people exiting from their homes and moving in a procession behind Kino to the pearl-buyers. Steinbeck writes that "the houses belched people; the doorways spewed out children," and in so describing, he has effectively attributed certain desired characteristics both to the town itself and to the people who live there.

In summary then, more than not, *The Pearl* portrays the basic battle for survival in which all living creatures must engage. Man in Steinbeck's novel is stripped of his own proverbial goodness and is depicted as susceptible to his greed, his destructiveness, and his basic instincts. As such, he is reduced to his primitive animality and must engage in the same battle for survival as do the roosters, pigs, and birds introduced in the first paragraph of the novel. To reinforce this basic comparison between man and animal, a comparison so essential to the theme of the novel, Steinbeck deliberately chooses language throughout the novel which will emphasize the animal-like actions and reactions of his characters. As a result, all living creatures exist on the same level, and all react to life in much the same manner.

SENTENCE STRUCTURE

In addition to selecting carefully the words he uses, Steinbeck effectively manipulates his sentence structure for emphasis and flow of ideas. For instance, he frequently uses the expletive phrase *it is* to emphasize a significant point. For example, in the first chapter, he prepares to introduce the scorpion by setting the scene and placing his characters. He then begins his important paragraph with the sentence, "It was a tiny movement that drew their eyes to the hanging box." Whereas he could easily have omitted the first two words of the sentence and not lost any meaning, Steinbeck seems intentionally to use the expletive phrase *it was* to emphasize the tiny movement and to draw effectively not only Kino's but our own attention to the hanging box. We find our curiosity aroused and will pay a little closer heed to what follows in an effort to discover exactly what has caused the tiny movement. Steinbeck is then ready to introduce the dreadful scorpion which will strike Kino's son, and, as an author who is extremely sensitive to the effects of language, he does so in a masterful sentence. Kino and Juana freeze in their positions, and Steinbeck writes: "Down the rope that hung the baby's box from the roof support a scorpion moved slowly." Because unpunctuated, the sentence reads smoothly from beginning to end. Suspense is created, for Steinbeck saves the scorpion for the end of the sentence. The alliterative *s* sounds near the end of the sentence echo and draw out the continuous movement of the scorpion, and beginning the sentence with the adverb *down* creates an inescapable sense of downness. Finally, because of Steinbeck's deliberate word order, the sentence has a rhythm which requires the reader to move just as *slowly* through the sentence as does the scorpion down the rope.

The Flawed Narrative Structure of *The Pearl*

Roy Simmonds

Roy Simmonds finds *The Pearl* flawed, charging that it is too complex a work for such a slight story line. Simmonds writes that Steinbeck loads the novel with too many distinctive narrative forms: cinematic, realistic, and fabular. According to Simmonds, the cinematic quality is too intrusive and artificial, and the realistic narrative is not credible. *The Pearl* does not work on the fabular level either because, unlike a pure parable that expresses a single moral truth, *The Pearl* explores myriad moral propositions. Simmonds is the author of *John Steinbeck: The War Years, 1939–1945*, from which the following critical essay is excerpted.

The Pearl suffers as a novella because of the cinematic point of view imposed on it, which is, here and there, too intrusive.

Most of the action of the novella is seen through Kino's eyes, and almost the whole of the book's emotional thrust is expressed through Kino's simple and limited conscious thoughts. At the very beginning of the story, for example, there is a description of Kino awakening in his hut in the morning: Kino's eyes become the camera lens through which the reader sees precisely what Kino sees, in the same way that the audience in the cinema sees precisely what the director of the film wants it to see:

> Kino's eyes opened, and he looked first at the lightening square which was the door and then he looked at the hanging box where Coyotito slept. And last he turned his head to Juana, his wife, who lay beside him on the mat, her blue shawl over her nose and over her breasts and around the small of her back. Juana's eyes were open too. Kino could never remember seeing them closed when he awakened. Her dark eyes made little reflected stars. She was looking at him as she was always looking at him when he awakened.

The Kino viewpoint is not, however, uniformly sustained throughout the book. There are occasions when intentional digressions are introduced—such as, to quote two examples, the scene in the doctor's bedroom in Chapter 1, and the second paragraph of Chapter 2 with its description of the tiny marine life of the beach—but there are also those other occasions when Steinbeck slips awkwardly from the subjective viewpoint of Kino to an objective authorial viewpoint, as in the scene when the trackers and the horseman stop in the road opposite the spot where Kino is hiding:

> When the trackers came near, Kino could see only their legs and only the legs of the horse from under the fallen branch. He saw the dark horny feet of the men and their ragged white clothes, and he heard the creak of leather of the saddle and the clink of spurs. The trackers stopped at the swept place and studied it, and the horseman stopped. The horse flung his head up against the bit and the bit-roller clicked under his tongue and the horse snorted. Then the dark trackers turned and studied the horse and watched his ears.

Although perfectly acceptable in cinematic terms, such an abrupt switch from subjective to objective viewpoint, when the reader has been conditioned to the idea that Kino's range of vision is severely restricted so that he can see only the legs of the trackers and of the horse, is momentarily distracting and ruptures our complete identification with Kino, if not our continuing awareness and appreciation of his predicament.

STEINBECK'S USE OF THEME MUSIC

While most of the cinematic techniques reflected in *The Pearl* are perfectly acceptable, and in some cases work wonderfully well, the use of "theme music" as a means of pointing to a mood or to an emotion or to concentrate on a particular object does seem rather artificial on the page. The aural repetition of certain musical themes by way of background music is markedly more unobtrusive but more insidiously effective in registering on the subconscious of the individual members of a cinema audience than is the stark repetition of printed words on the eyes of the reader. As Steinbeck had told [Pascal] Covici, he laid great emphasis on the importance of the musical score, and in *The Pearl* he introduces the Song of the Family, the Song of Evil, the Song of the Enemy, the Song of the Pearl That Might Be, the Song of the Undersea, and, of course, "the music of the pearl" itself.

This use of "music" is a re-use of the experimental device Steinbeck had employed far more subtly in *Cannery Row* during the episode when Doc discovers the drowned young girl in the La Jolla tide pool. It was a device he was to use again in the "tones" or "voices" that Doc hears within himself in *Sweet Thursday*."

Despite these reservations, *The Pearl* works more successfully as a novel in its own right than does either *The Moon Is Down* or his third published play-novel, *Burning Bright*. The confinement to stage setting interiors that bedevil those two books disappears in the far-ranging outdoors action of *The Pearl*. Yet the freedom Steinbeck enjoyed to open up the original basic parable posed its own problems, and these problems he did not entirely solve. He weighed himself down with so much specific action, so much elaboration of character, not to mention metaphor and inner meaning, that the simple storyline became perilously overburdened.

The elimination of stagecraft artificiality does not, on the other hand, automatically ensure that a more realistic atmosphere will pervade a work. It should be borne in mind that Steinbeck consistently referred to *The Pearl* as a parable. Any attempt to consider the book solely as a work of realism presents immediate difficulties, for arguably there is some justification in contending that Steinbeck failed to establish his characters in a completely believable set of circumstances. To believe in the reality of the whole, it is necessary to believe in all, or (at the very least) most of, the component parts. In short, it has to be accepted without question that, against all odds, Coyotito would have survived the scorpion sting, that Kino could so successfully and easily have attacked and killed the four men hired to rob and murder him, and that one bullet fired more or less blindly toward the cave entrance from thirty feet or so below could have blown off the top of Coyotito's head as he lay under a blanket close against his mother's back.

A FLAWED ENDING

Perhaps even more importantly from the realistic point of view, the principal problem Steinbeck did not and could not solve was to reach a credible ending for the book. He was, of course, saddled with that ending, for it does provide the whole *raison d'être* of the story. But what has been altered disastrously in Steinbeck's overelaborated version are the

DISPARATE REVIEWS

The publication of The Pearl *generated as many disparate critiques as there were book reviewers. The following two review excerpts testify to this diversity of critical opinion. The first review appeared in the* Chicago Sun Book Week *in 1947; the second appeared a year later in the* Spectator.

[*The Pearl*] is a parable. Hence it's rather short. But it's long enough to give Steinbeck an opportunity to bring into play some of his most distinctive talents, notably his knack for infusing a kind of dynamic rhythm and lyric quality into his prose, his dramatic use of the vernacular, and rare ability to convey direct sensuous impressions.

The narrative is of a sort, moreover, that gives him a beautiful chance to express his well-known sympathy for society's underdogs and indulge his fondness for primitive and symbolical characters. . . .

Despite its rather rudimentary plot, *The Pearl* succeeds in stirring the emotions profoundly. It succeeds, too, in giving eloquent testimony with regard to Steinbeck's integrity and maturity as a literary artist.

• • • • •

Mr. Steinbeck is not quite at home with his old Mexican "folk" story—"fake" would be better—of Kino, his wife Juana and their child Coyotito. Kino finds a great pearl, tries to sell it, learns that merchants cheat, keeps the pearl, commits murder, runs away with his family, is hunted and when the baby is killed comes home and throws the pearl away. Mr. Steinbeck tries hard to be simple, but he only manages to be embarrassing: "Coyotito whimpered and Juana muttered little magics over him to make him silent." The book is really a fine example of what the Germans call *erstklassiger Kitsch* [firstclass kitsch]. It is difficult to find an adequate English translation for these withering words and kinder perhaps not to try.

Ralph Habas, *Chicago Sun Book Week*, November 23, 1947.
Stevie Smith, *Spectator*, October 29, 1948.

events leading up to the casting of the pearl back into the sea. In the original legend, the Indian boy did not kill anyone. He had no wife, no child, no house, no boat. Indeed, he had no identifiable position in the community. He existed conveniently as a single human being without apparent family ties and without possessions. After he had been attacked and beaten and tortured, there was a simple logic to his gesture in throwing the pearl, the cause of all his troubles, back into the sea: he just wanted to be left alone and to return to his old, uncomplicated, peaceful, if poverty-ridden, way of life. But, as [critic Warren] French has pointed out, in Steinbeck's version "too many loose ends remain unresolved." Steinbeck has encumbered Kino with so many possessions at the beginning of the story, has established his position in the tiny fishing community so firmly, that it has become impossible for Kino, by the simple act of returning the pearl to the sea, to regain the dubious "Eden" of his former way of life. It cannot be ignored that his boat, his "bulwark against starvation," has been destroyed, his baby is dead, and his relationships with his wife and his brother and the other villagers have been radically and irretrievably altered by what has happened. Although the implication is that Steinbeck wants his readers to accept all this as a satisfactory, if not a happy, conclusion to the story, it is, as French has maintained, no ending at all. It does not seem possible that Kino would be content to return to the environment from which he imagined he had escaped, nor can it be accepted that he would have been welcomed back unreservedly by those whom he had, in his briefly assumed position of superiority, been forced to leave behind in his obstinate search for wealth. And what of the four men he has killed? Are not the pearl dealers going to exact some sort of revenge, even if they cannot now get their hands on the pearl by fair means or foul? It is surely significant that at the conclusion of the book of all the things Kino desired when he first held the pearl in his hand there is only one that he now possesses—indeed, it is his only possession: a rifle, a symbol of violence that he has acquired by violence. Kino will have to defend himself with it. There is more blood to be shed— ultimately, some time or other, inevitably Kino's own. The logical ending of the story is in that future tragedy and death.

MULTIPLE MORAL TRUTHS

It follows that if, after due consideration, the book does not convince as a work of realism, it should be accepted as the parable Steinbeck says it is. Here, again, is another problem. In its purest form, a parable (or fable) expresses a single moral truth. In *The Pearl* there is a multiplicity of possible moral truths or quasi-moral propositions: that, in the words of St. Matthew, "What is a man profited, if he shall gain the whole world, and lose his own soul?"; that one should accept one's preordained social station in life and not presume to aspire above it; that pride goes before a fall; that greed is never rewarded; that happiness cannot be achieved through material wealth; and so on. Because Steinbeck has so loaded the story with detail, with various examples of human behavior, any one of these questionable conclusions, or any combination of them, can be regarded as equally valid. Steinbeck has left the reader with an open-endedness that is not only unsatisfactory on the realistic level but on the fabular level as well.

Steinbeck's own subsequent ambivalent attitude toward *The Pearl* is clearly expressed in the brief introductory note to the published book. "If this story is a parable," he suggests, "perhaps everyone takes his own meaning from it and reads his own life into it." It is possible that Steinbeck did consciously set out to make the work mean all things to all men. On the other hand, there could have been a confusion of intent in his mind, so that when the work was finished, as a letter to his agents at the time implies, he felt that he had failed in what he had set out to do.

If he did fail, he certainly did not fail because *The Pearl* is too simple a work, but because it is too complex a work. In it, he tried to encompass not only three quite-disintinctive narrative forms (cinematic, realistic, and fabular), but also an overwhelming preponderance of identifiable symbols, metaphors, and philosophies for so slight a tale. There are strong echoes of the Bible, Greek tragedy, and Faustian legend all present in the manner of the telling. If Steinbeck *has* succeeded, as most critics would maintain, in creating a considerable work of art, he has possibly done so by default. What, above all, is certain is that a work that can raise so many passions in its critics, generate so many contradictory interpretations, elicit so much praise for the beauty and clarity of its prose, and give immense pleasure to countless millions of discerning readers cannot be judged a failure.

Proportioning in *The Pearl*

Roland Bartel

Steinbeck's proportioning in *The Pearl*—the amount
of space Steinbeck allocates to various elements of
the story—provides the reader with important clues
with which to interpret the work, explains Roland
Bartel. A quantitative approach, according to Bartel,
leads the reader directly to the primary theme—
man's struggle against a predatory community—and
prevents undue emphasis on secondary matters.
Bartel was a professor of English at the University of
Oregon in Eugene.

One of the most useful guides in interpreting and teaching a
novel is often overlooked. In our haste to discuss imagery
and symbolism, subtleties of character, and the nuances of
language, we frequently neglect an important preliminary
step: a close look at the proportioning in a novel, the amount
of space allocated to various episodes, characters, and
themes.

Beginning with a quantitative approach to a novel should
lead us directly to the central theme and prevent us from
giving disproportionate emphasis to secondary matters. . . .

Although an awareness of proportioning is helpful in
studying works in all genres, it is of particular value in setting priorities for interpreting the longer literary works. A
close look at proportioning in John Steinbeck's *The Pearl*, for
example, should help us set aside many popular misinter-
pretations. In each of the six books the protagonist is Kino,
and the antagonist is the community around him. In the first
book Kino is repulsed by a corrupt and sensual doctor, and,
significantly, he cuts his hand when he defiantly strikes the
doctor's gate. In the second book he seeks and finds the
pearl that will enable him to purchase medical care for his

Excerpted from Roland Bartel, "Proportioning in Fiction: *The Pearl* and *Silas Marner*,"
English Journal, vol. 56, no. 4 (April 1967). Copyright 1967 by the National Council of
Teachers of English. Reprinted with permission.

son. In the third book Kino dreams of the new life made possible by the pearl but has to contend immediately with three predatory agents of the community, the priest, the doctor (no longer needed since Coyotito is recovering), and the assailant in the night. In the fourth book he defies the pearl buyers and the whole structure of the community, as his brother reminds him, and fights off another would-be intruder. In the fifth book after preventing his wife from throwing the pearl back into the sea, he kills an assailant and discovers that the community has destroyed his boat and his house. In the last book the community pursues him in the persons of the trackers, destroys his son, and drives him to the extremity of throwing the pearl back into the sea.

KINO'S STRUGGLE

Finding the pearl gives Kino a vision of a better life—respectability through a marriage ceremony and better clothes, improved earning power and self-protection through a harpoon and a rifle, but most important of all, an education for Coyotito. His son's literacy will protect him from the priest, the doctor, and others he suspects of taking advantage of his own illiteracy. Kino's dream of a better life is not presented as something unworthy or degrading; he is entitled to the good things his new wealth makes possible, and his ambitions are reasonable and in character. But at every step the community frustrates his attempt to fulfill himself. Although he now has the resources to improve himself legitimately, he is beaten down by the community at every turn.

The more the community threatens to deprive him of his sudden good fortune, the more Kino determines to obtain fair value for the pearl. The pressure from the community becomes so great and his resistance becomes so resolute that he is driven to equate the pearl with his soul; achieving the way of life represented by the pearl becomes an obsession with him.

When Kino is pursued by the trackers in the sixth part, he never questions the rightness of his action; he has no feelings of remorse, no second thoughts about the decision he has made. When he returns to La Paz with his wife, the pearl, and the body of his slain son, he is not pictured as having completed a journey into self-knowledge or experienced a spiritual rebirth. Why does he return? He returns, because he has been crushed. Having been shorn of the possibility of a better life (the pearl is meaningless without Coyotito), he cannot surrender, or flee, or make a deal for his safety. He returns, because it is futile to go on. Killing the first three trackers from the community does not give him a clear road ahead . . . but multiplies the crimes for which he will have to answer. He returns because he has deep roots in his native community and strong loyalties to its traditions. The person who had too much self-respect even to think of taking someone else's boat when his own had been destroyed retains his pride at the end by facing his defeat defiantly. He has lost everything, but he makes certain that his exploiters do not benefit from his loss. We may recall that when Kino defied the pearl buyers he realized that he had left his old world but had not yet entered a new one. When his brother told him he had defied a whole way of life, Kino replied that his son must have a chance and that *that* is what his enemies are striking at. Now that his enemies have struck, he returns to the scene where his aspirations were first aroused and challenged, not to admit the error of his ways, but to show that in his defeat he will not surrender to his antagonists the object of their greed, the object for the possession of which they killed his son.

KINO'S TRANSFIGURATION

The only possible support for the idea that Kino may have experienced some sort of victory comes from a sentence concerning the townspeople who observe the return of Kino and Juana near the end of the book: "The people say that the two seemed to be removed from human experience; that they had gone through pain and come out on the other side." But these are the same neighbors who, on the day the pearl was found, anticipated that they would remember the day for years to come as the day of the great marvel, the day they saw Kino transfigured. They are also the people who, we are told in the headnote, retold all stories only in terms of "good and bad things and black and white things and good and evil things and not in-between any where." No, the neighbors transfigured Kino because that was their tradition. It is more likely that they admired his defiance than that they discerned any transformation of character, something completely unprepared for in the novel. The things that Kino sees in the pearl before he discards it—reminders of the ugly experiences he has just passed through—symbolize the success of the community of exploiters in warping the means to a new and better life into a means of death. To say that in throwing the pearl into the sea Kino is symbolically divesting himself of false values is to sentimentalize his character by attributing to him qualities which are inconsistent with his earlier actions and statements. This interpretation also implies that Kino was wrong and the exploiters were right, something hardly in harmony with the rest of the novel. We should not forget that Kino hangs on to his newly-acquired rifle when he returns to La Paz.

ESTABLISHING THEME

The proportioning tells us that from the first chapter to the last, from the efforts to get Coyotito healed to the struggles to get a fair return for the pearl, Kino is at the mercy of the exploiters. The primary theme is the heroic struggle of a pearl diver who unsuccessfully fights a predatory community in his determined effort to fulfill the hopes aroused by his finding of the pearl. Others in Kino's class are resigned to their fate, but he is not. His experience parallels that of minorities in our own society who, once given a vision of self-respect and self-fulfillment, will risk their lives rather than permit their vision to fade.

Once this primary step of establishing the theme by paying close attention to the proportioning in the novel has been completed, we can interpret other elements in the novel with greater confidence and profit. We can observe that Kino's struggle for self-respect is supported by his strong sense of tradition and family loyalty, that his intuitive but unverbalized awareness of the dangers he is facing is suggested by the songs of evil and the songs of joy, and that other lyrical elements in the novel enrich the background for the action. We can note the significance of Kino's splitting his knuckles in expressing his hatred for the doctor, whose class has exploited Kino's class for 400 years, and of Kino's several times holding the pearl in his injured hand. We can discuss the haze of the estuary, the sleight-of-hand tricks of the first pearl buyer, the animal imagery at key places in the story, and the animal-like existence of the main characters at various times. We can note the correlation of the pearl and Coyotito: the pearl was first sought to save Coyotito's life, then is linked to Coyotito in meaningful ways (he whimpers, for example, when Kino announces that he will keep the pearl at all costs), and finally becomes the reason for his death rather than his life. We can see the importance of the first chapter in establishing the courage and capacity for quick action on the part of Kino and Juana, the very deep feelings that underlie their actions, their extreme poverty that makes the finding of the pearl such a momentous experience for them, and the possible foreshadowing in the pearl-like glitter on the scorpion's tail. The sea as a source of life in this and many other literary works can now be discussed in proper context. The biblical echoes in the title can also be examined. In Matthew 13:45–56, a merchant who seeks pearls finds one of great price (the kingdom of heaven) and sells everything else to obtain it. Kino also finds a pearl of great price through which he hopes to obtain a material heaven, but the irony is that he not only cannot sell the pearl but has to renounce it after it has deprived him of both his old way of life and the new life he had envisioned.

CHAPTER 3

A Critical Selection

READINGS ON
THE PEARL

The Role of the Mountains in *The Pearl*

Louis Owens

> To critic Louis Owens, the mountains in *The Pearl*
> are thematically and symbolically central to Kino's
> story. Indeed, Steinbeck infuses the mountains with
> an atmosphere of foreboding, mirroring the virtu-
> ally unconquerable troubles that beset Kino. More-
> over, it is in the mountains that Kino must face the
> dark forces that threaten him. Owens maintains that
> ultimately Kino achieves greatness through his will-
> ingness to journey into the dark mountains and
> confront the unknowable. Owens is the author of
> *John Steinbeck's Re-Vision of America*, which in-
> cludes the following essay.

The Pearl has generated more contradictory criticism than any
other work by Steinbeck. It has been passed over lightly and
condemned as "defective" and a betrayal by such an esteemed
Steinbeck critic as Warren French; and it has been called a "triumph, a successful rendering of human experience in the
round" by another, Howard Levant. As Sydney J. Krause has
pointed out in a succinct summary of *Pearl* criticism, the novel
"has been regarded on the 'black' side as defeatist, negativistic,
pessimistic, somber and pathetic, tragic, a study in futility, and
a rejection of the promise of salvation; while, on the 'white'
side, it has been taken as heroic, a rejection of naturalism, a re-
establishment of the meaning of existence, a personal victory,
and a triumphant preparation for salvation." The novel has
been read as a teleological parable and as a non-teleological
parable. It has been called allegory and morality.

THE KEY ROLE OF SETTING

In spite of the minor critical furor caused by this novel, critics have paid surprisingly little attention to the key role of

Excerpted from Louis Owens, *John Steinbeck's Re-Vision of America* (Athens: University of Georgia Press, 1985). Reprinted by permission of the author.

setting—specifically the mountains—thematically and symbolically in the novel.

It is likely that the mountains into which Kino and Juana flee in *The Pearl* are modeled after a range of mountains that Steinbeck and Ricketts discovered during their expedition to the Sea of Cortez. In *The Log from the Sea of Cortez*, Steinbeck recounts a hunting trip for the elusive *borrego*, or bighorn sheep. Steinbeck and Ricketts are invited by a rancher on the Mexican coast "to go into the tremendous and desolate stone mountains to camp and hunt." As they approach the rugged mountains, they pass over a "rolling, rocky, desolate country . . . toward the stone mountains, steep and slippery with shale." The terrain leading to the base of the peaks is described as a "fantastic" country, a term once again echoing the surreal description of the landscape within the Chinaman's eyes in *Cannery Row*. It is covered with "thorned bushes and trees" which "crackled with heat," and "poison bushes." Once in the mountains, the party enters a "deep cleft in the granite mountains," a cleft in which a tiny stream "fell hundreds of feet from pool to pool." The resemblance between these mountains and those in *The Pearl* is readily noted. However, these apparently real mountains quickly take on a nightmare quality beyond their natural desolation when we encounter them in the novel, and they come to represent a symbolic landscape much like that described in "Flight," a landscape within which Kino, like Pepé Torres in "Flight," must make his stand against the dark forces that pursue him. Like Pepé, Kino will make his stand within the very jaws of the mountains, and like Joseph Wayne in *To a God Unknown*, Kino will experience his rebirth of consciousness through an experience of death in a kind of *omphalos*—the stream at the heart of the world.

There are marked similarities between the stories of Pepé and Kino. Both of these characters begin their stories as "naturals"—Pepé as a bumbling child of nineteen and Kino as a naïve child of nature, completely unsophisticated—and both are closely identified with animals and undergo a process of dehumanization in the course of the stories. Both men lose the possessions of their fathers and virtually all possessions that tie them to civilization: Pepé loses his father's coat, hat, rifle, and horse, and Kino his house and, most important, his boat. Both Pepé and Kino kill a man and must flee because of this, and both kill as if by accident;

Pepé's knife seemed to act of its own volition, and Kino has killed in darkness: "I was attacked in the dark . . . and in the fight I have killed a man. . . . It is all darkness—all darkness and shapes of darkness." And, most important, though both men flee to the mountains instinctively to avoid death, it is death that they find there, and the experience makes Pepé a man and Kino, as we shall see, a man transcendent and set apart.

SYMBOLIC LANDSCAPE

In "Flight" death and the impenetrable mystery of the western mountains are symbolized by the darkness that permeates the story, from Pepé's black knife to the dark watchers. In *The Pearl* darkness again symbolizes the experience of death that awaits Kino and Juana, but perhaps more significantly, darkness in this novel stands for the unknown that surrounds the Indians, the unknown within which death is an integral factor. Our first knowledge of Kino comes in the first sentence of the novel: "Kino awakened in the near dark." In the state in which we meet him, Kino is more akin to the animal life that surrounds him than to the men who inhabit the town. His life consists of instinctive responses, responses embedded deeply within the collective unconscious of his people. He and Juana are the primal pair in the prelapsarian [time before the fall of man] garden of their village, awakening to "a morning like other mornings and yet perfect among mornings." Though the first dawn of the story comes blindingly, Kino will soon begin a descent into darkness that will lead him ultimately into the total darkness of the climactic scene in the heart of the mountains.

DARK FORCES

Even before the pearl brings its threat into the book, darkness is an ominous force in this novel. Before Kino rises, for example, we are told that he covers his nose with his blanket to protect himself from "the dark poisonous air" of the night. Later, we learn that Kino has his people's instinctive "fear of dark and the devils that haunt the night." After Kino has found the pearl, the threat of darkness grows as he sinks more deeply into his "dark night of the soul." His struggles with the evil forces all occur at night, and when his hut is burned he is forced to hide from the daylight in the darkness of Juan Tomás's house. As Kino is forced more and more to confront the unknown forces of darkness, he becomes increasingly a creature of the night. After he has killed the first "dark one," we are told that the "light made him afraid"; and when Kino and Juana finally set off for the north, they leave "quietly in the dark." They travel at night until they are forced into the mountains, and the final scene of violence and death is acted out in darkness broken only by the rising moon.

Throughout the novel, the forces of darkness remain faceless and nameless. We are never told who or even what the shadows are that attack Kino or who has sent them, and, though we may speculate, we are not told why the dark ones pursue Kino and Juana into the mountains. Kino's first attacker, within the hut, is described as a "dark thing," and when Kino is attacked the second time, we are told that "he could feel the dark creeping things waiting for him to go out into the night." Kino does dare to go out into the night, and when he has grappled with and killed something at last recognizably human, the body lies on the ground "with dark shiny fluid leaking from his throat." [Critic] Joseph Fontenrose says of Kino's pursuers, "They are dark, never clearly seen, mysterious, as if Pepé's invisible pursuers in 'Flight' were one with the dark watchers." In *The Pearl* the dark watchers have indeed become one with the pursuers; they represent the abstract evil that has fallen upon Kino, as if distilled from the "dark poisonous air" of the night which Kino feared from the beginning. When Kino dares to go out into the night, literally and symbolically, he is challenging the unknown, prodding dark fears into life as palpable and confrontable "things."

NON-CAUSAL PHILOSOPHY

By dehumanizing the forces that attack Kino, Steinbeck also de-emphasizes causality and emphasizes what he and Ricketts called in the *Log* "the non-causal or non-blaming viewpoint." The mysterious threat that the dark figures represent from beginning to end in the novel is simply a stark fact with which Kino must come to terms once he has broken from the old order, once he has, in Juan Tomás's words, "defied not the pearl buyers, but the whole structure, the whole way of life." Steinbeck makes it clear that Kino has indeed isolated himself in a new realm of existence where he must face alone the forces which oppose him: "He had lost one world and had not gained another. . . . Kino had lost his old world and he must clamber on to a new one."

In accordance with this "non-causal or non-blaming viewpoint," Fontenrose has pointed out that "everything in *The Pearl* is in-between," that it is difficult to see only black and white, good and evil. Fontenrose suggests that "this is a non-teleological parable: This is the way things are." If we try to affix the blame for Kino and Juana's situation, we find it to be very difficult. Is the threat to the family the result of the fact that Juana prayed for the pearl rather than directly for Coyotito's cure? Is the result of the pearl buyers' attempts to cheat Kino or the fault of the unknown figure who rules these lesser men? Or is it Kino's fault for daring to defy the structure and disrupt the harmony of the "colonial animal" which is his people and village? We cannot trace a clear blame for Kino's fate to any specific cause or individual or group in the novel; the fate in store for Kino and Juana simply *is*, and Kino must grapple with it in the form of the dark pursuers. If he fails he, like Pepé, will perish; if he succeeds he will live and he will be greater than before. As it was for Pepé, Kino's struggle is the struggle of all men that Steinbeck defined in *East of Eden;* his antagonists are "shadows, perplexities, dangers without names or numbers . . . a faceless death." These shadows and perplexities, which exist in the darkness surrounding all of the Indians, become for an instant "described and recognizable" when Kino confronts them, and there can be little doubt that in the end Kino is "a man set apart from other men."

It is in the mountains that Kino must face his greatest test, and our first view of the mountains in *The Pearl* emphasizes their mystery: "A vision hung in the air to the north of the city—the vision of a mountain that was over two-hundred miles away, and the high slopes of this mountain were swaddled with pines and a great stone peak arose above the timber line." Like Elizabeth and Joseph in *To a God Unknown*, and like Pepé in "Flight," Kino and Juana flee instinctively toward the high place "as nearly all animals do when they are pursued." It is in the mountains that Kino will undergo a rebirth of consciousness precipitated by an overwhelming experience of death, and in this first view of the stone peak Steinbeck carefully juxtaposes an image of birth—"swaddled with pines"—with the image of death pervasive in his early writing, the stone mountains.

THE OMINOUS MOUNTAINS

Steinbeck's description of the mountains into which Kino and Juana flee, though probably suggested by the mountains described in the *Log*, mirrors his description of the surreal coast range in "Flight." With phrases like "the naked granite mountains, rising out of the erosion rubble and standing monolithic against the sky," Steinbeck infuses the landscape with an atmosphere of foreboding. As in "Flight," there are "long outcroppings of granite" and "bare unremarkable stone," and, finally, there is the strong suggestion that, like Pepé, Kino and Juana and Coyotito may be devoured by the desolate mountains: "The sun moved downward toward the bare stone teeth of the mountains, and Kino set his direction for a dark and shadowy cleft in the range." Like Pepé, Kino is fleeing directly into the jaws of the mountains, and though Kino and Juana will survive, four lives will be left within these jaws.

The barren and ominous terrain mirrors Kino's inner desolation. Earlier, Kino has confessed that the pearl has become his soul, and in the mountains we are shown the corruption which has beset that soul:

> He looked into the pearl to find his vision. "When we sell it at last, I will have a rifle," he said, and he looked into the shining surface for his rifle, but he saw only a huddled dark body on the ground with shining blood dripping from its throat. And he said quickly, "We will be married in a great church." And in the pearl he saw Juana with her beaten face crawling home through the night. "Our son must learn to read," he said frantically. And there in the pearl Coyotito's face, thick and feverish from the medicine.

In this rather heavy-handed passage, the pearl reflects the real values of those things for which Kino has wished. The rifle can bring nothing but sorrow to Kino and his family—what need has a fisherman for a rifle? In the course of the novel, Kino receives a rifle and with it a crushing tragedy. Likewise, the desire for marriage in a "great church" is simply a value foisted upon the Indians by the church of the corrupt priest, a priest who is an integral part of the system that oppresses and exploits the Indians without mercy. And finally, the image of Coyotito suffering from the doctor's trickery suggests that were Coyotito to become educated, he would become part of the system outside the unified whole of the village, that system represented by the corrupt priest, the doctor, and the pearl buyers.

Unfortunately, the question of Kino's desire for an education for Coyotito cannot be answered this simply, for it poses one of the central problems of the book: Is Kino justified in wanting a thing so different and so disruptive to the harmonious "whole" in which we find him in the opening pages of the novel? Or, in the end when Kino and Juana return to the village and repudiate the pearl and its values, are we to see this as a sign that Kino was wrong from the beginning? Howard Levant has suggested that Kino progresses from "personal and rather selfish desires . . . to wholly selfless, idealistic thoughts of sending Coyotito to school." It is not quite so easy to distinguish between Kino's desires, however, for his desire for Coyotito's education is not completely selfless—through Coyotito's education Kino dreams of being freed from the grasp of the men in the town: "My son will read and open the books, and my son will write and will know writing. And my son will make numbers, and these things will make us free because he will know." Steinbeck helps his reader to resolve this dilemma, however, by making it unmistakably clear that Kino's desire to free himself and others from their entrapment is to be admired. There can be no doubt that Kino is trapped. When the doctor works his trickery on Coyotito, Kino suspects that it is a trick, but he is helpless to protect his son: "He was trapped as his people were always trapped, and would be until, as he had said, they could be sure that the things in the books were really in the books." And there is no doubt about Steinbeck's attitude toward Kino's challenge to the order: "For it is said that humans are never satisfied, that you give them one thing and they want something more. And this is said in disparagement, whereas it is one of the greatest talents the species has and one that has made it superior to animals that are satisfied with what they have." Kino's desires for a rifle and a church wedding, and even, perhaps, for his son's education, may be delusive, but the courage to have them not only forces Kino "through the horizon into a cold and lonely outside," but makes him superior in the end to the animals with which he and his people are identified and superior to the rest of his people who do not act upon such desires. Ironically, when Steinbeck writes that "all of the doctor's race spoke to all of Kino's race as though they were simple animals," the doctor's race seems fairly correct in its assessment, for the Indians' lives are much like those of animals—ruled primarily by instinct and habit. By the end of the novel, Kino and Juana will be forever risen above this level.

Kino's Impotence

From the beginning of the novel, Kino struggles to escape from an entrapment that seems as inexorable as fate. Our perspective as we watch Kino is precisely the same as Kino's when, early in the novel, he watched "with the detachment of God while a dusty ant frantically tried to escape the sand trap an ant lion had dug for him." Throughout the novel, Kino is the ant in the trap, and the higher he climbs the more the sides of his trap close in upon him. In this respect, critics who have read *The Pearl* as naturalistic are correct. From the beginning to the end, Kino, like the other Indians, is at the mercy of forces—social, economic, hereditary—which he cannot defeat. The naturalistic images and symbols of the book deny Kino the possibility of overcoming these forces— he is the ant in the trap, the small fish in the estuary preyed upon by the greater, the mouse hunted by the nighthawk. He is completely ineffectual in his attempts to protect his true pearl, Coyotito. When he sees the scorpion threatening the baby, he tries to intervene but is too late. All he can do is crush and stamp the enemy "until it was only a fragment and a moist place in the dirt." Similarly, he demonstrates his impotence in the face of the doctor's callousness by smashing his fist against the iron gate. And, in the end, in a scene prefigured by the scene with the scorpion, Kino leaps to prevent the rifleman from endangering the baby but is again too late and Coyotito is killed. Once again, all that Kino can do is crush the enemy just as he had crushed the scorpion—in a frenzy of killing. In a non-teleological sense, the evil forces that overpower Kino simply *are*, like the "sadness of the stomach" Pepé's mother warned of.

TELEOLOGICAL THINKING

Kino is also trapped by shortsighted teleological thinking which assumes that the pearl will provide the ability to buy "things" that will bring greater happiness. In this thinking Kino is like the others in his village and town. The Indians, however, are especially vulnerable to this kind of thinking because they have no experience against which to judge the values suggested by the pearl. In their innocence, the Indians are non-teleological by nature; they simply accept things as they are. Kino's story is that of a man emerging from a non-teleological state of innocence (prepearl) into the teleological world of misleading values ("things" the pearl can buy), and of his final transcendence to a *conscious* recognition of non-teleological values in which the pearl loses its power. The greed and violence that Kino encounters within himself and others are based on the teleological assumption that the pearl can cause happiness. In order to be immune to the temptations of this kind of thinking, Kino must work from ignorance through experience to a conscious awakening. With the death of Coyotito, Kino awakens to the value of the true pearl he has lost, and his enslavement to the "pearl of the world" ends.

During the dark hours of his enthrallment to the pearl, Kino told Juana, "Believe me . . . I am a man," and Steinbeck had added, ironically undercutting this statement, "And his face grew crafty." After the loss of Coyotito and the gain of a new world-vision, Kino is more than a man just as he was less than a man before. He and Juana return to the village as transcendent beings: "The people say that the two seemed to be removed from human experience; that they had gone through pain and had come out the other side; that there was almost a magical protection about them." The symbols of their experience of death return with them: "The sun was behind them and their long shadows stalked ahead, and they seemed to carry two towers of darkness with them. Kino had a rifle across his arm."

Contrary to what Warren French has suggested, Steinbeck is not simply saying here that one *can* go home again. Nor can we easily agree with Levant's assertion that, when Kino hurls the pearl back into the sea, Kino and Juana "renounce the lure of 'the world' and can reenter their former Eden, forgiven." Krause convincingly argues that "the grand gesture of a public renunciation is in itself about as forceful a demonstration of moral action as any of Steinbeck's characters ever make," but the serious import of this novel cannot be found in Krause's claim that "by this dramatic public admission of personal wrong, the man has truly reclaimed his soul." And Steinbeck is not merely telling us here, as Fontenrose suggests, that "this is the way things are." When Kino and Juana return, the villagers, including Kino's brother, shrink from them in fear; they cannot "reenter their former Eden, forgiven," for they are forever set apart by their experience. Nor do they need to be forgiven, for they have been made greater than before by the knowledge they have gained. No longer will Kino and Juana be at the mercy of the pearl buyers and the corrupt town, for the values represented by the town have been discarded at the instant of Coyotito's death. Kino and Juana have been thrust into a world apart from the innocent garden of the village, and the casting away of the pearl represents not a public admission of wrong but simply the casting aside of something which no longer has any personal value.

TRIUMPH IN DEFEAT

The Pearl is a parable of man achieving greatness through the courage to challenge the unknown. Though there is never any chance that Kino will defeat the powers that oppose him, he triumphs in defeat. He illustrates Steinbeck's claim in *The Grapes of Wrath* that "man reaches, stumbles forward, painfully, mistakenly sometimes. Having stepped forward, he may slip back, but only a half step, never the full step back."

In *To a God Unknown* Joseph Wayne achieved his triumphant vision of his relationship with the "whole" at the moment of death. Pepé Torres, in "Flight," achieved a kind of transcendence into the "whole" represented by the mountains at the moment that he "stood up in the dark" to confront the unknown and unknowable forces pursuing him. This, too, has been Kino's triumph. Kino has gone into the night and into the dark mountains to confront the unknown, leaving the security of his known, safe world. In so doing, Kino has joined the ranks of Steinbeck's Questers, those who journey into the western mountains on a quest to know that which is unknowable except by "*being* it, by living into it."

Biological Descriptions in *The Pearl*

Masanori Tokunaga

Prior to his writing *The Pearl*, Steinbeck researched and wrote *The Log from the Sea of Cortez* and *The Sea of Cortez: A Leisurely Journal of Travel and Research*, books that detail his scientific studies in the Gulf of California. According to Masanori Tokunaga, *The Pearl* reveals Steinbeck's increasing knowledge of biology, an interest that intensified during his experience writing these books. Indeed, Steinbeck infuses *The Pearl* with elaborate descriptions of living things. Even when describing inanimate things, Steinbeck imparts animalistic imagery, as when he describes Kino's town as having "a nervous system and a head and shoulders and feet." This critical essay was first published in Japan by the Kyushu American Literature Society.

In reading Steinbeck's works, it is necessary to pay attention to his interest in biology. First I should like to briefly examine how he became interested in biology; next I should like to see how his interest in living creatures is shown and what the biological descriptions mean in *The Pearl*.

Salinas, California, where he was born and brought up, is a beautiful place which is rich in natural scenery and living things. As a boy, Steinbeck was familiar with nature, walking about and smelling the odor of wild life. His interest in biology, fostered in Salinas, was accelerated as he chose biology to study at Stanford University and became acquainted with Edward F. Ricketts. [According to E.W. Tedlock Jr. and C.V. Wicker:]

> John Steinbeck's interest in biology, and particularly in marine zoology, is of long standing. Presumably his studies at Stanford University awakened an interest which was intensified by his long friendship and association with Edward F. Ricketts, formerly a professional collector of biological specimens at Monterey.

From Masanori Tokunaga, "The Biological Descriptions in *The Pearl* and Their Meanings," *Kyushu American Literature*, vol. 16 (1975). Reprinted with permission.

It is very significant that he met Ricketts. It seems that he had a friend who had a common interest in biology.

In *The Sea of Cortez* they compared their trip to Darwin's voyage on the *Beagle*, saying that their method was somewhat like that of Darwin. References to Darwin resulted in non-teleological thinking, from which perhaps Steinbeck's attitude derived from seeing things as they are.

He looked into tide pools and examined marine living things, wondering about their organisms and their ability to live. In doing so, he began to think of human beings as being formed of the same kinds of cells as the marine animals. This resulted in primitivism or his view of seeing human beings as animals. Tide pools showed him the way of "the group-man theory," one of the features in his writing.

Thus he gained and intensified his interest in biology or living things.

In *The Pearl*, which was published a few years after *The Sea of Cortez*, he expressed his knowledge of biology and by using it, made this work varied in technique and content.

BIOLOGICAL DESCRIPTIONS

Descriptions of marine animals or plants are often found in [*The Pearl*]. Sometimes he depicts them elaborately in details and scientifically.

> The gray oysters with ruffles like skirts on the shells, the barnacle-crusted oysters with little bits of weed clinging to the skirts and small crabs climbing over them. An accident could happen to these oysters, a grain of sand could lie in the folds of muscle and irritate the flesh until in self-protection the flesh coated the grain with a layer of smooth cement. But once started, the flesh continued to coat the foreign body until it fell free in some tidal flurry or until the oyster was destroyed.

Sometimes he heightens the descriptions to the level of lyrical poetry:

> And the pearl settled into the lovely green water and dropped toward the bottom. The waving branches of the algae called to it and beckoned to it. The lights on its surface were green and lovely. It settled down to the sand bottom among the fern-like plants. Above, the surface of the water was a green mirror. And the pearl lay on the floor of the sea.

The contrast is remarkable in the above two passages. Although he talks about marine life in the former, he is a sheer scientifist and in the latter, he is a lyrical poet.

Marine animals or plants add color and variety to this work. Oysters, algae, crabs, and other marine living things play their parts in making readers feel as if they were seeing a technicolor film and in giving something lively to this work. If Steinbeck had not been interested in marine animals or plants and had not introduced them into this work, it would have become just an ordinary story. Biological descriptions and song are mixed together and are an effective audio-visual technique as "the little secret melody of the pearl."

A TOWN COMES ALIVE

Even when he describes lifeless things, he takes a biologist's view and this adds something lively and peculiar to this work.

> The news stirred up something infinitely black and evil in the town; the black distillate was like the scorpion, or like hunger in the smell of food, or like loneliness when love is withheld. The poison sacs of the town began to manufacture venom, and the town swelled and puffed with the pressure of it.

I feel as if the city had life and spat something. It seems that this expression is suitable for symbolizing the evil of the city. In the following description towns themselves have nerves and emotions.

> A town is a thing like a colonial animal. A town has a nervous system and a head and shoulders and feet. A town is a thing separate from all other towns, so that there are no two towns alike. And a town has a whole emotion.

This seems to have come from his observation in *The Sea of Cortez:*

> There are colonies of pelagic tunicates which have taken a shape like the finger of a glove. Each member of the colony is an individual animal, but the colony is another individual animal, not at all like the sum of its individuals.

His interest in marine living things shown in *The Sea of Cortez* is shown in *The Pearl,* too, which makes the town alive. Peter Lisca refers to this description like this:

> *The Pearl* brings together several more of Steinbeck's techniques and preoccupations as a writer. His tendency to think of groups as unit animals is revealed in his description of the "nerve lines" and "units" of a small town.

ALTERNATING TENSION AND RELAXATION

Steinbeck recognizes animality in human beings as "some animal thing" in Kino, which is connected with his view of thinking of man as an animal. In "Flight" he refers to animality in human beings in Pepé's "reduction to the state of a wild animal."

In the scene of Kino and Juana's flight, he arranges the descriptions of animals and plants effectively in accordance with the tension and relaxation of Kino and Juana's feelings.

Kino and Juana take "the rutted sandy road that led through the brushy country toward Loreto where the miraculous Virgin has her station." They set out on a secret journey to seek a place where they can live in peace. But this hope is broken with the death of Coyotito. In fleeing, they are full of tension, which is stressed by the sudden appearance of coyotes, owls or some large animal.

Moreover, the author describes the desert country which "was waterless, furred with the cacti" and "with the great-rooted brush." It is a wasted, lifeless land with few living things. Kino and Juana's flight "was panic flight" and this landscape matches their mental state.

With the appearance of a little spring their fear disappears. At this place all living things are full of life and find comfort. Steinbeck's way of describing living things is detailed here and he repeats the same elaborate descriptions of the living things in the desert in his later work, *Travels with Charley.* This induces me to think of his interest in biology again.

Kino and Juana seem to find comfort here, too, but their momentary rest is broken by the trackers. Again they are full of anxiety which is accentuated by the twittering of tree frogs and the ringing of cicadas. But the tree frogs and cicadas become silent when Coyotito and the trackers die and their flight is ended. They are full of grief instead of tension at the death of Coyotito. They cannot see "the miraculous Virgin" but can find "themselves" by throwing away the pearl which has now become ugly.

I think the author's technique of alternately using tension and relaxation, symbolized by living things, is useful to make this flight scene more exciting and varied.

I have seen biological descriptions in *The Pearl,* and his other works. [Critic] Edmund Wilson writes:

> Yet there is in Mr. Steinbeck's fiction a substratum which remains constant and which gives it a certain weight. What is constant in Mr. Steinbeck is his preoccupation with biology.

Family Dynamic in *The Pearl*

Linda Wagner-Martin

In *The Log from the Sea of Cortez*, Steinbeck tells of a Mexican boy who finds a pearl that, albeit exquisite and of great value, ultimately poisons the boy's existence. Steinbeck introduced key changes in his retelling of this basic story in *The Pearl*. According to Linda Wagner-Martin, Steinbeck reworked the original tale to reflect his personal situation, primarily by making Kino into a husband and father. By extending the story to include a wife and child, Steinbeck adds richness and complexity to the plot, creating an acutely vulnerable protagonist whose travails reach tragic proportions. The following essay by Wagner-Martin is excerpted from her introduction to the Penguin edition of *The Pearl*.

As [Steinbeck] thought about the pearl story [telling of the Mexican boy who finds a pearl of great value] . . . the legend seemed much too simple. In the *Sea of Cortez* narrative, the boy finding the pearl was intent on using it for money to buy drink, sex, and clothes. The tragedy in this version of the tale was that the pearl dealers in La Paz (the ironically named Village of Peace) would not give him a reasonable price for the pearl, and after realizing that he was the victim of their collusion, he buried the jewel. Owning such valuable property, he became the target for attack, and that night he was beaten. The next night, when he stayed with a friend, both boys were beaten; later, when he traveled away from the village, he was again tracked and beaten. So he returned to La Paz, dug up the pearl, cursed it, and threw it into the sea. In Steinbeck's words, "He was a free man again with his soul in danger and his food and shelter insecure. And he laughed a great deal about it." While a reader might question what was comic about an endangered soul and insecure living, one of Steinbeck's points was that, as a single man, his protagonist could take chances with life. His existence was not threatened by his giving up the fortune.

What was important about the legend as Steinbeck recalled it is that the boy had the sense to get rid of the object that was going to cost him his life. The original pearl story, then, is a parable of materialism, an example of the dangers of prosperity in a culture that thinks nothing of killing for money. But the pearl story as Steinbeck wrote it several years later is different, and it shows how complex his own state of mind was at this time of conjunction of war experience, Hollywood film experience, material success from *The Grapes of Wrath* and other ventures, with all the good things tempered radically by the deaths he had observed in the theater of war, as well as by the death of his marriage. The year 1944 was a time of personal change for John Steinbeck, and he was apprehensive about that change.

His personal situation influenced his creation of *The Pearl*. When Steinbeck wrote his version of the story, he made the young man into the older Kino, a responsible married man with a wife and child to provide for. Kino is probably named for Eusebius Kino, the Jesuit missionary and explorer in the Gulf region (it was he who proved that lower California was a peninsula—a *Baja*—rather than an island). In *Sea of Cortez*, Steinbeck had shown his knowledge of many of the explorers and missionaries, both Mexican and American, involved with the settlement of the Baja. That journal too has a spiritual overlay, as Steinbeck used it to explore several sets of principles for leading a good life.

Juana, the name he chose for Kino's wife, means "woman," and as such she becomes the answerer, the solace for her husband's disappointed idealism. As in his earlier fiction, particularly in the characters of Ma and Pa Joad in *The Grapes of Wrath*, Steinbeck drew male and female as complementary characters, with the woman having wisdom, common sense, and authority to balance the man's more wistful and sometimes unrealistic hopes. With tempered sympathy, Steinbeck acknowledges that Kino is obsessed with hanging on to the pearl, and that in equating it with his pride, he fails to see that his more useful role toward his family would be protecting them. When he confesses that the pearl has become his soul, Kino admits that he will endanger his family rather than relinquish his prize, and his abuse of Juana when she tries to get rid of the pearl illustrates his growing fanaticism. In that unexpected violence, Steinbeck shows how far from any Jungian individuation Kino's wealth has taken him—he is a monster of a male ego, not a caring and supportive husband. But behind Kino's obviously rash behavior stands the tranquil wife, who watches over him while he sleeps and starts the fire each morning. Though all-knowing and all-caring, Juana in her role as submissive wife does not have enough power to make Kino listen to her warnings.

Juana is also the mother of Kino's most prized possession, his son, Coyotito. Kino says that his wish in finding the pearl and recognizing its value is that Coyotito be educated, that he become a savior figure to lead his village out of the abject poverty in which it exists. For most of the novella, Kino is so filled with this urgent hope that he does not hear Juana's counsel; her role becomes significant only near the end of the tragic tale, when the formative events have already occurred. Rather, Kino is led by an internal song he calls "The Song of the Family," a melody that haunts him with its sound; "this is safety, this is warmth, this is the *Whole*." In some respects, *The Pearl* is a parable of a personal journey toward that indivisible unity, or "wholeness," described by Carl Jung. Kino's dilemma over the pearl may also be read as a metaphor for his struggle to claim his unconscious self and integrate the "shadow" side, the femaleness within his male identity. He must come to see life, at least in part, as Juana does.

Narratively, Steinbeck complicates the parable of the pearl of great price when he adds the vulnerability of the baby, first introducing the child's helplessness in the scorpion scene. No matter how attentive his parents are, no matter that both are within arm's reach of the child, they cannot prevent the insect's biting him. Once bitten, the child becomes the object of attention, an icon to test people's values. The villagers know his worth to Kino and Juana; they understand Juana's desire that he receive formal medical treatment, and they follow the young family to the house of the doctor. But when the white man refuses to treat the child, they also understand that money is his only god, and Kino obviously is poor. Later, when the doctor reverses his position and comes to Kino's hut (only to poison the child and then give him an antidote—both visits serving as the means for him to look for the pearl's possible hiding place), the community also understands that duplicity. During the night, the physician sends someone to steal the jewel. He has put the family's real jewel, their son, at risk in the process of enabling himself to profit from Kino's simple luck.

Extending the plot to include a child, then, creates a kind of vulnerability that putting either Kino or Juana in danger would not have conveyed. The perversion of sheer innocence, and its ravishment, sets in motion a dynamic like that of medieval morality plays. Steinbeck, well read in medieval texts, created his own version of the fourteenth-century alliterative poem *Pearl,* an elegy by the anonymous poet for the death of his daughter before she was two years old. In this 1212-line poem, the sorrowful poet persona sees a vision of his child as the young woman she would have become. As a result of the dream or mystical experience, he plunges into a river, attempting to join his child in her blessed, heavenly state. His journey, a plunge into the dark night of the soul, leads to his awakening, and to his eventual acceptance of the child's loss. The poem closes with the poet's renunciation of his earthly pain: "Upon this hill this destiny I grasped, / Prostrate in sorrow for my pearl. / And afterward to God I gave it up." As the poet moves past his understandable grief for the loss of his child, he comes to realize the limits of human will and the confines of human consciousness. He places his trust in God.

Steinbeck transfers the resonance of the medieval legend to his own *Pearl* and forces the reader to see that Kino's journey to safeguard the pearl becomes an allegory of spiritual struggle. In the course of protecting the precious jewel, Kino kills a man who is nameless, formless, a kind of evil in himself—and he does so without remorse. As he takes more and more evil into his own behavior, finally killing three more men as he rationalizes that he must perform these acts to guard the pearl that will improve the lot of his family, Kino endangers his own morality. The explorations of his namesake in the Baja wilderness are tame compared with Kino's exploration of the levels of human sin. In the shifting value of the pearl—from great material worth into an objectification of sheer evil—Steinbeck leads the reader to see that its eventual loss will be a necessity.

Again, by focusing on the family dynamic, Steinbeck adds

AN AUTOBIOGRAPHICAL READING OF *THE PEARL*

The seed story of The Pearl, *which Steinbeck recorded in* The Log from the Sea of Cortez, *featured a young, single Indian boy. According to critic Joseph R. Millichap, Steinbeck's transformation of this character into a husband and father supports an autobiographical reading of the novel.*

The story [of the pearl in *The Log From the Sea of Cortez*] matches the basic outline of *The Pearl*, though Steinbeck makes several major changes, changes significant in an autobiographical sense. In the original, the Mexican fisherman is a devil-may-care bachelor; in *The Pearl* he becomes the sober young husband and father, Kino. Steinbeck himself had just become a father for the first time when he wrote the novelette, and this change provides a clue to the autobiographical nature of the parable. The original bachelor thought the pearl a key to easy living; Kino sees it as a means to create a better way of life for the people through an education for his baby son, Coyotito. If Coyotito could read and write, then he could set his family and his people free from the social and economic bondage in which they toil. Again the allegory suggests the author's life; he believed material success as a writer would bring the opportunity to study, to write, to create. Kino is ignorant of the dangers of wealth, and *The Pearl* is the tale of how he matures by coming to understand them. Steinbeck, too, matured from his youthful innocence as he felt the pressures of success.

Joseph R. Millichap, *Steinbeck and Film*, 1983.

both life and complexity to his narrative. Kino is not an individual Everyman; he is husband and father as well as man. In fact, being parents complicates all decision making for both Kino and Juana: Kino justifies his wanting the money from the pearl to better his son's life; his is no selfish desire. Relinquishing the jewel consequently becomes almost impossible, for to give up the money the pearl will bring means relegating Coyotito to the kind of life he and his family have always known. But in a cyclic way, with so much hope invested in Coyotito, his vulnerability frightens both his parents. Juana insists that the doctor see him; Kino, at the farthest edge of his imagining—with the idea that his son could receive an education—begins to understand personal fear. His premonition of wrongdoing, that he has taken on something much larger than he can control, starts with that hopeful idea.

Kino's older brother, Juan Tomás, is another important addition to Steinbeck's reworking of the original legend. The reactions of Juan Tomás support Kino's almost inarticulate recognition of what is happening to him, giving the reader a way to verify that Kino's understanding is accurate. Because Steinbeck's setting for *The Pearl* is almost dreamlike, and certainly unspecific as to geographic location, to provide this confirming voice is necessary: This is a community, a set of people, a family; and yet for all the strength of their unity, they cannot stave off the evil that haunts Kino once he possesses the pearl. Juan Tomás as the older brother has a wider understanding: He knows that Kino has been cheated, but he also knows that they have all been cheated, through history. His is the voice of reason, the voice of continuity, and the voice of caution. Early in the novella he warns Kino that he has no model for what he is attempting—and he concludes that such ambition must be wrong, for no one else has attempted such an act.

Despite this warning, however, Juan Tomás is loyal to Kino; and Steinbeck is careful to set the inner circle of family and friends against the broader, suspect community. People in the inner circle want Kino to succeed, even though their imaginations are stunned with the thought of his undertaking. They serve as a Greek chorus to echo, and reify, Kino's thoughts. They literally follow him to see what he is going to do next, and their presence (and the muffled echo of their words as they explain to those farther away what is happening) serves as validation. In form, then, as well as in the undercurrent of doom that pervades *The Pearl*, Steinbeck creates the effects of the Greek tragedies he admired.

CHAPTER 4

Characters in *The Pearl*

READINGS ON
THE PEARL

The Pearl: Character Analysis

Martha Heasley Cox

Like many great writers, Steinbeck took his plots
from other stories. Martha Heasley Cox describes
how Steinbeck found material for *The Pearl* in a true
story about an Indian boy and a pearl. This seed
story contains several characters that appear transformed in *The Pearl.* Cox presents a portrait of each
of these characters, including minor characters who,
although less prominent, add color and meaning to
the narrative.

In *The Log from the Sea of Cortez,* Steinbeck's account of the
scientific junket which he, Ed Ricketts, and their companions made in 1940 to the Gulf of California, Steinbeck tells of
their visit to the fascinating and venerable city of La Paz. Indians are proud to have been born in that city with its magic
carpet name, renowned throughout the area and once the
great pearl city of the world. Steinbeck recounts an event
which occurred there in recent years, a story of an Indian
boy and a pearl, which, he says, seems to be true, though "it
is so much like a parable that it almost can't be," a story that
"is far too reasonable to be true."

> An event which happened at La Paz in recent years is typical
> of such places. An Indian boy by accident found a pearl of
> great size, an unbelievable pearl. He knew its value was so
> great that he need never work again. In his one pearl he had
> the ability to be drunk as long as he wished, to marry any one
> of a number of girls, and to make many more a little happy
> too. In his great pearl lay salvation, for he could in advance
> purchase masses sufficient to pop him out of Purgatory like a
> squeezed watermelon seed. In addition he could shift a num-
> ber of dead relatives a little nearer to Paradise. He went to La
> Paz with his pearl in his hand and his future clear into eter-
> nity in his heart. He took his pearl to a broker and was of-
> fered so little that he grew angry, for he knew he was cheated.
> Then he carried his pearl to another broker and was offered

Excerpted from Martha Heasley Cox, "Steinbeck's *The Pearl*," in Tetsumaro Hayashi,
ed., *A Study Guide to Steinbeck: A Handbook to His Major Works* (Metuchen, NJ: Scarecrow Press, 1974). Reprinted by permission of the publisher.

the same amount. After a few more visits he came to know that the brokers were only the many hands of one head and that he could not sell his pearl for more. He took it to the beach and hid it under a stone, and that night he was clubbed into unconsciousness and his clothing was searched. The next night he slept at the house of a friend and his friend and he were injured and bound and the whole house searched. Then he went inland to lose his pursuers and he was waylaid and tortured. But he was very angry now and he knew what he must do. Hurt as he was he crept back to La Paz in the night and he skulked like a hunted fox to the beach and took out his pearl from under the stone. Then he cursed it and threw it as far as he could into the channel. He was a free man again with his soul in danger and his food and shelter insecure. And he laughed a great deal about it.

Steinbeck completed the manuscript for *The Log from the Sea of Cortez* in 1941, using the two journals he and Ed Ricketts had kept on the trips. Not until 1944, four years after the visit to La Paz, did Steinbeck write his version of the "true story.". . .

The brief original story of the pearl contains several characters, all of whom Steinbeck uses in some form in his novella: an Indian boy, a number of girls, dead relatives, pearl brokers, a friend, attackers, and pursuers. The unnamed Indian boy is transformed into Kino, named, as the Priest tells him, for a great man and a great father of the church, who "tamed the desert and sweetened the minds of thy people." That man was the seventeenth-century Jesuit, Eusebius Kino, a missionary and explorer in the Gulf region. Kino, Steinbeck's protagonist, is a young married man with a child, who is respected in the community. He has black hair; a thin, coarse moustache; and warm fierce eyes. Over his clean white clothes which have been washed a thousand times, he wears an ancient blanket and a large straw hat, properly tilted. A fisherman and pearl diver, he owns his own canoe, inherited from his father and grandfather before him, and his brush hut, but can offer the doctor what is seemingly his total wealth otherwise—eight ugly, misshapen almost valueless seed pearls in payment for treating his son.

KINO: A PORTRAIT OF COURAGE

Kino is a quiet sensitive man, who has great strength and courage. His sigh of satisfaction is to him conversation, and his account of the future he sees in the pearl is the longest

speech Juana has ever heard him make, causing her to wonder at his courage and imagination. He listens continually to
an inner music, not knowing whether he alone or all of his
people hear it. He speaks softly to his timid dog and always
touches his canoe tenderly. When he leaves the cave to attack the pursuers, he lays his palm on Coyotito's head in
farewell and touches Juana's cheek. But he fights fearlessly
when his family is threatened, snarling and baring his teeth
when he destroys the scorpion; leaping, striking, and spitting at the dark thing in his house; and moving with the
strength of a terrible machine as he kills the three pursuers.
Yet when he encounters the brokers, his only defense is a
slight slitting of the eyes, tightening of the lips, and a reti-
cence. Angered at their collusion, he strides away, with
blood pounding in his ears, and decides, though he has
never been away from home and fears strangers and strange
places, to go to the capital to sell his pearl. Beset by conflict-
ing emotions of fear and anger when he approaches the doctor, his actions show the ambivalence he feels: his lips draw
tight in anger as he knocks but he simultaneously raises his
other hand to take off his hat. After his public shaming when
the doctor refuses to see him, he . . . can only strike out. In
the absence of his adversary, he strikes the gate such a
crushing blow that the blood flows from his split knuckles.

Kino possesses a native shrewdness which serves him
well: he instinctively knows his dramatic effect when bar-
gaining with the broker; he hears the music of evil when the
priest visits; he refuses to give the pearl to the doctor for
safekeeping; he knows that the pearl is valuable because of
the attempted thefts.

Kino changes after the discovery of the pearl. He feels
trapped by his own ignorance and by the doctor's greed and
duplicity. He becomes cautious and suspicious, fearing
everyone, knowing that even the gods are hostile to his
plans. His brain burns "even during his sleep." He is determined, however, to give his family a future, to see that his
wishes for them, which are both modest and admirable,
have a chance for fulfillment. He resists, therefore, Juana's
pleadings that he throw the pearl—and the future he envisions—back into the water. When she defies him, and tries
to throw the pearl away herself, he beats her brutally before
he turns away in sick disgust. Later, however, he decides
twice to sacrifice himself for his wife and son, once through

surrender to the pursuers, once as a decoy to lead the trackers on while Juana hides with Coyotito. Only Juana's insis-
tence that his surrender would be futile, since they would all
be killed anyway and she wishes to stay with him, prevents
either action. Finally, when Coyotito is dead, he returns to
the city, as "dangerous as a rising storm."

JUANA: THE IDEALIZED WOMAN

The number of girls the Indian boy wishes to marry or "to
make . . . a little happy" coalesce in Juana, whose name
means "woman" and who, in the novella, is Kino's only romantic interest. She has dark eyes which make "little reflected stars" and wears her black hair in two braids tied
with ribbons. When the story opens she wears an old blue
skirt and torn shawl, but changes to her wedding skirt and
waist for the trip to the pearl brokers.

Juana is the idealized woman, obedient, respectful, cheer-
ful, patient, and courageous. She is a good mother, caring for
Coyotito and reassuring him with soft songs to make him
feel warm and safe. When Coyotito is wounded, it is Juana
who sucks the poison from his puncture, then insists that he
be treated by the doctor. She keeps the baby quiet on the
flight until, after many hours of silence, his murmuring cry
alerts the pursuers to their presence. Then it is her "keening,
moaning, rising, hysterical cry . . . of death" that reveals
Coyotito's fate to Kino and to us.

A helpmate to Kino, she shows surprising strength and
courage. In the canoe she rows like a strong man and with-
stands hunger and fatigue almost better than Kino himself.
Her prayers in time of trouble are a mixture of ancient magic
and a Hail Mary. It is she who first senses the evil in the
pearl and twice pleads with Kino to destroy it. When he refuses, she tries to throw it back into the water herself. She
tends Kino when he is wounded, rushes to help when he is
attacked, and drags the body of the man he murdered into
the bushes. It is Juana who then decides that they must flee.
On their return "her wide eyes stared inward" and she was
"as remote and removed as Heaven."

KINO AND JUANA

The relationship of Kino and Juana undergoes subtle
changes as the story progresses, indicated, at least in part, by
their relative standing or walking positions: when they go to

see the doctor, Juana walks first, carrying Coyotito, with
Kino following behind; on the way to and from the pearl brokers, Kino goes first and Juana follows; when they begin
their flight, Kino again leads, while Juana, carrying the
baby, trots after him. But in times of sorrow, shame, or renunciation, they stand or walk side by side: when they are
humiliated by the doctor they stand side by side in rejection;
when they return to La Paz, they walk not in single file but
side by side; when Kino throws the pearl into the water, they
stand side by side for a long time.

Whatever the specific and local cultural and ethnic patterns which at least help determine their relationship, they
are also influenced by the man-woman syndrome, a pattern
of behavior dictated by their, and perhaps Steinbeck's, atti-
tudes toward their respective sexes. The narrator tells us
that though Juana is puzzled by the differences between a
man and a woman, she knows, accepts, and needs them. In
reply to her repeated pleading that he destroy the pearl,
Kino's face grows crafty and he refuses, saying twice, "I am
a man"; and Juana is silenced, "for his voice was command."
When, exercising her "quality of woman" for reason, caution, and preservation, she attempts the deed herself the next
morning and receives a severe beating for her efforts, she
neither resists nor tries to protect herself. When Kino said "I
am a man," that "meant that he was half insane and half
god"; and "Juana had need of a man; she could not live without a man." Though in her "woman's soul" she knew she
would be destroyed, she would follow him without question,
and sometimes her "quality of woman . . . could cut through
Kino's manners and save them all." She does preserve the
family unit twice on the flight; once, when she goads Kino
out of surrender, and again, when he takes strength from
her refusal to stay behind while he goes on alone. In the
final scene, she softly refuses when he offers her the pearl;
maintaining the man-woman roles, she leaves the gesture of
renunciation to him.

Hints of catharsis, on their emergence from the valley of
the shadow of death after the sacrifice of their firstborn in
the mountains, occur when the narrator tells us that as Kino
and Juana return, walking side by side, they seem removed
from human experience, as if they "had gone through pain
and had come out on the other side" and "that there was almost a magical protection about them."

OTHER CHARACTERS

Other characters mentioned in the seed story are the pearl brokers, the pursuers who were presumably also the attackers, a friend, and dead relatives. Four pearl buyers appear in Steinbeck's version, without names but with distinct personalities, all differentiated in some way from one another, but all alike in their desire to perform their duty to their common employer, conniving to convince Kino that the pearl is of little value and to buy it as cheaply as possible. In the novella, the attackers, even more ominous because they are without form or name, are assailants who creep in the night, identified as "the sound" or "the thing." The pursuers on the flight are three, the dark horseman carrying the rifle and the two inhuman trackers, who scutter, crawl, and whine "like excited dogs on a warming trail." The closest parallel to the friend of the seed story is Kino's brother, Juan Tomás, who offers counsel about selling the pearl and caution about defying the way of life of the fishermen. Like the Indian boy's friend, Juan Tomás shields Kino in his home after Kino has killed his unknown assailant. Although the dead relatives the Indian boy "could shift . . . a little nearer Paradise" do not appear in Steinbeck's version, the Masses of the seed story are mentioned in the sketch of the doctor, whose dead wife "if Masses willed and paid for out of her own estate could do it, was in Heaven."

The doctor; Coyotito; Juan Tomás's wife, Apolonia, and their four children; the doctor's servant; the priest; the neighboring fishermen; the four beggars; the shopkeepers; and the Chinese grocery store owners are not suggested in the seed story. Some are only supernumeraries; some more; but all add color and verisimilitude to the story.

The most fully developed is the doctor, a fat and lazy man, who is cruel and avaricious. A member of a race which has starved, robbed, frightened, and despised Kino's people for nearly four hundred years, he is the chief antagonist of the novella. His clothing, a Parisian dressing gown of red watered silk; his appearance, eyes which rest in puffy little hammocks of flesh, and mouth drooping with discontent; his breakfast, chocolate and other sweets served in silver and fine china—all delineate his position and character and differentiate between his life and Kino's. Though the doctor battens on the suspicion, fear, and ignorance of the fishermen, he tends their sick only when assured of ample recompense, feigning the need for his services when none exists, and practicing subterfuge rather than the healing art to attain his ill-gotten wealth.

COYOTITO

Coyotito, the baby, serves chiefly as catalyst. His scorpion sting necessitates the visit to the doctor and, in turn, the search for the great pearl. Kino's desire to give his son an education is a major reason for retaining the pearl. Juana's concern for his welfare and safety help define her role as woman, even in defiance of her husband. His death is the ultimate pain, the death of hope, which leads to the return of his parents and the rejection of the pearl. His name, the diminutive of the Mexican-Spanish word for Coyote, derives from the Nahuatl word "coyotl." Steinbeck emphasizes the connection when he has one of the pursuers speculate that the baby's cry from the cave may be a coyote, for he has heard "a coyote pup cry like a baby.". . .

Critics have interpreted *The Pearl* in a number of ways. It has been called a search for values, man's search for his soul, a study of the vanity of human wishes, the struggle of one man against a predatory community, a lesson showing that man must stay in his own niche and not encroach on others, and, most often, a rejection of materialism. Though the omniscient narrator guides the reader toward an interpretation or, at least, toward several thematic statements, Steinbeck, in the prefatory comment, invites every reader to take his own meaning from the story, to read his own life into it.

Juana: A Woman of Worth

Mimi Reisel Gladstein

Mimi Reisel Gladstein chides Steinbeck critics who
have ignored or diminished the significance of Juana
in *The Pearl*. To Gladstein, Juana stands as the most
admirable character, representing a composite of the
best qualities of the archetypal female. As evidence,
she demonstrates how Steinbeck purposefully infuses
Juana with positive attributes: Throughout the story,
the unwavering Juana symbolizes strength, devotion,
courage, and wisdom, representing the nurturing
qualities of women and also exhibiting a strong survival instinct. Gladstein is a professor of English and
theater arts at the University of Texas at El Paso. She
has published numerous articles on Steinbeck and
other American authors.

Many critics have pointed out that American male novelists,
even our most prestigious writers, have difficulty creating
fully human females. Feminist critics emphasize the negative portraitures that result from what [author] Leslie A.
Fiedler calls the American male novelist's inability to draw
"convincing portraits of women." While not disagreeing
with this statement in the main, I would point out that not
enough attention has been paid to the supra-human female
stereotype in much of American fiction. This is not to say
that she is any more "real" than her deprecated sisters, but
she does stand as a positive symbol for human endurance
and survival in works by authors who project a generally
pessimistic world view.

Perhaps the personification of this indestructible woman
in American fiction is Steinbeck's Ma Joad. Certainly, the obstacles she must overcome and the indomitability she ex-

From Mimi Reisel Gladstein, "Steinbeck's Juana: A Woman of Worth," in Tetsumaro
Hayashi, ed., *Steinbeck's Women: Essays in Criticism*, Steinbeck Monograph Series, no.
9 (Muncie, IN: The Steinbeck Society of America and Ball State University English De-
partment, 1979). Reprinted by permission of the publisher. Footnotes in the original
have been omitted in this reprint.

hibits are unequalled. But Ma Joad is not an anomaly in Steinbeck's work. Though much critical attention has been paid her, little note has been taken of other indomitable Steinbeck heroines, such as Juana in *The Pearl.* After Ma Joad, she is the most positively depicted woman in Steinbeck's works. Flatly characterized, Juana never quite emerges as a real person, but since the story is a fable or a parable, a realistic portrayal is hardly required. What is significant is that in this parable, which reduces the human situation to essentials, the woman is the most admirable, most indomitable character.

READINGS BY CRITICS

Unfortunately, few critics pay even cursory attention to Juana's role in the fable. Lester Jay Marks mentions her only in passing, noting that the pearl causes Kino "a spiritual estrangement from his wife." This oversight is all the more glaring since he is careful enough to note Steinbeck's interdiction that in such parables "there are only good and bad things and black and white things." Marks equates Kino with the good, an equation hardly borne out by a careful reading of the novel. Kino is the learner, the pilgrim in search of values, while Juana is a constant. Though Kino must learn of the evil that greed engenders, Juana is instinctively aware from the beginning. Her values never change; she is, from beginning to end, devoted to the preservation of her loved ones, man and child.

Warren French observes that Steinbeck changed the original legend on which *The Pearl* is based to include Juana; the anonymous boy in the legend is unmarried. However, French does not pause to consider the implications of this addition to the meaning of the fable. If all Steinbeck wished to transmit was the greed and frustration that result from material gain, there would be no need to include a courageous and enduring woman. None of the characters in the original version is an exemplar of positive values. The Indian fisher-boy wants the gains from the pearl's sale only to enable him to loaf, to drink, to have many girls, and to buy his way to heaven. Steinbeck's version enlarges the scope of the message to include man, woman, and child. In the altered tale the message is seemingly more pessimistic than in the original. Kino not only loses the pearl, but the baby (his future) dies, and his boat (livelihood) is smashed. What relieves the dark future and differentiates Steinbeck's message from the message of the original is the character of Juana. Though Kino loses the pearl, he retains her loyalty and devotion, and although the baby dies, Juana's presence presages future children.

Like other critics, Harry Morris subjects *The Pearl* to a thorough and careful scrutiny, and though he realizes the importance of Coyotito, the baby, he barely mentions Juana. And neither James Gray nor Richard O'Connor finds her characterization worthy of note. Considering the importance of her function and the care with which Steinbeck develops her positive qualities, this is a lamentable oversight on the part of discerning critics.

An Indestructible Woman

Conceivably she could have been depicted as a carbon copy of Kino, mirroring his moods and desires, much like Hemingway's submissive heroines, or she could have been portrayed as an avaricious wife like the one in the [Grimm's] fairy tale, "The Fisherman and His Wife." Since she is neither and since her character is carefully developed, Steinbeck obviously had a positive function in mind in creating this indestructible woman. Specifically, as the heroine in this fable Juana symbolizes the positive and nurturing qualities of woman, the omnipresent mother, always on guard to protect her own. Steinbeck imparts this idea through Juana's eternal watchfulness: "Juana's eyes were open too. Kino could never remember seeing them closed when he awakened. Her dark eyes made little deflected stars. She was looking at him when he awakened." The image here is of a sky goddess overseeing her wards. Later in the novel, when they are being pursued, Juana guards Kino's sleep.

In addition, Juana's devotion to the family is symbolized by the music Kino hears in her presence and the three-note ancient song she sings. The song's message is "this is safety, this is warmth, this is the *Whole*." When that safety is threatened, Juana's reaction sounds the echo of the family song in Kino's perception: "And Kino saw her determination and the music of the family sounded in his head with a steely tone." It is Juana's determination that goads Kino into going for the doctor when the doctor has refused to come.

Throughout the fable Juana is seen as the more effectual of the two. When the baby is bitten, it is Juana who sucks out the poison, while "Kino hovered, he was helpless, he was in the way." When the doctor will not come, it is Juana who through the force of her indomitable will practically effects the finding of the pearl which causes the doctor to come. Juana's is a magic of intense will: "her face set, rigid, and her muscles hard to force the luck, to tear the luck out of the god's hands, for she needed the luck for the swollen shoulder of Coyotito." Ironically, she successfully forces the luck, but it turns out to be bad luck.

A SOURCE OF STRENGTH

Throughout the story Juana is the epitome of strength and devotion, but not, however, of an unquestioning doglike or servile variety. When Juana's better judgment decides that the pearl will only bring disaster, she defies Kino and tries to throw it away. She is beaten for her trouble. Defeated in her attempt to dispose of the pearl, she resigns herself to standing by Kino: "Juana, in her woman's soul, knew that the mountain would stand while the man broke himself, that the sea would surge while the man drowned in it." Implicit in the passage are feminine qualities of eternity in nature. Both the mountain and the sea are symbols for the archetypal feminine and, like the mountain, Juana endures though Kino's actions nearly break him and result in the death of Coyotito. That Juana stands not just for herself but for all womankind is emphasized by the narrator, who states, "Sometimes the quality of woman, the reason, the caution, the sense of preservation, could cut through Kino's manness and save them all." The quality of women that saves the world from the impetuous shortsighted manness is the survival instinct.

But Juana does more than just survive, she is a source of strength. When Kino confronts the pearl buyers, she bolsters him: "Kino was silent and watchful. He felt a little tugging at his back, and he turned and looked in Juana's eyes, and when he looked away he had renewed strength." When his determination flags, she encourages him. When the situation becomes dangerous, she will not leave him, though he tries to make her go: "He looked then for weakness in her face, for fear or irresolution, and there was none. Her eyes were very bright. He shrugged his shoulders helplessly then, but he had taken strength from her." But Juana's most incredible show of strength and wisdom comes at the end of the fable when all her worst dreads have been realized. When Kino gives her the pearl to throw away, she has the sensitivity to give it to him, to let him retain his sense of dignity.

Juana combines all the best qualities of wife and mother. Her portrayal is not, however, of the stereotyped traditional woman: feminine, submissive, weak, obedient. She is loyal and strong; protective, but not domineering. Her relationship with her husband is so elemental that the need for speech has been eliminated: "They had spoken once, but there is not need for speech, if it is only a habit anyway, Kino sighed with satisfaction—and that was conversation." This lack of verbalization, however, does not indicate a lack of knowledge or communication. Kino is very aware of the admirable qualities of his wife:

> Kino has wondered often at the iron in his patient, fragile wife. She, who was obedient and respectful and cheerful and patient, she could arch her back in child pain with hardly a cry. She could stand fatigue and hunger almost better than Kino himself. In the canoe she was like a strong man.

Juana is a composite of all the best qualities of the archetypal feminine. But for all her positive characteristics, Juana remains a flat character. As Woman she is nurturing and indestructible. As the symbol for womanhood she functions in admirable and beneficial ways, but as an individual woman, one Juana, wife of Kino, her personality never takes shape. As representative of her positive values, her presence presages affirmative future possibilities. A general criticism of Steinbeck has been the paucity of female characters in his works. While this is true, one must not ignore the significance of those who are there. Juana in *The Pearl* is a case in point.

Kino: The Ideal Man

Sunita Jain

According to Indian scholar Sunita Jain, Steinbeck believed that man functioned in two ways: as an individual and as a group animal. In her analysis of *The Pearl*, the protagonist Kino emerges as the ideal man, a group animal who retains his individuality and humanity despite devastating losses. Jain describes Kino's willingness to accept a painful reality—as his return to town suggests—and his defiance of a world that beats down the underdog as Steinbeck's ultimate expression of Kino's dignity and courage. Jain is the author of *John Steinbeck's Concept of Man: A Critical Study of His Novels*, from which the following is excerpted.

The Pearl, a novella, first published in *The Woman's Home Companion* of December, 1945, appeared in book form in 1947. The story in this novel is simple and simply told. However, like that of *Of Mice and Men*, the simple narrative has been imbued with cosmic significance. The hero struggles with the world for his right to exist with dignity. When denied, the hero, Kino, a fisherman in La Paz, defies the world by running away. The flight makes him realize that man alone is like a beast: he comes back to the world. The three movements of Kino's life correspond to the three parts of Steinbeck's concept of man—the individual, the social, and the ideal selves of man.

Kino, when we first meet him, is warm and content; the song of the family rages loud in his heart; he and Juana have no need for words; their communication is innocent of all strife. Contrasted to Kino's world is the world of the French doctor whose avarice and ignorant cruelty sends dead bodies to the church. And the doctor is a part of the town that has the pearl buyers and the priest in it.

Right from the start, it seems there are two camps in the story: man alone with his labours and innate dignity, and

Reprinted from chapter 9, "*The Pearl*," in *John Steinbeck's Concept of Man: A Critical Study of His Novels*, by Sunita Jain (New Delhi: New Statesman Publishing, 1979). Copyright 1979 by Sunita Jain.

man as vampire sucking at the vein of life, bringing about death and destruction.

Kino has need of the doctor when Coyotito is stung by a scorpion. Only he and Juana do not know that the doctor is a fraud. In their concern for their first born, he and Juana are weak, and they are weak because another world, a new world of possibilities, is there. But in transferring himself from one world to another, Kino suffers. His knuckles are split when he hits the doctor's door in rage, for the doctor refuses to look at the baby, pretending to be employed some place else.

Kino's Desires

The same drama repeats itself when Kino, fierce and angry, dives deeper than usual and stays down longer in order to find pearls. He comes back with the pearl of the world but the beauty of the pearl is dimmed and turns ulcerous because his heart is weakened. He wishes to marry Juana in a church and buy education for Coyotito. The irony here is extremely subtle. On the surface it seems that Kino wants the right things, but these things are right, or desirable, because of a new world of possibilities that has made itself attractive to men like Kino. The irony is that Kino and Juana are proper husband and wife in every sense of the word; they are married in body and soul. Yet Kino wants a social recognition to this marriage, and a religious sanction. His desire is clearly to please the new world and its priest rather than man or God; he also wants Coyotito to learn so the boy will have a chance. Again, the chance that he wants for the boy is in the new world. He desires to educate his son because he is dazed by the glitter of this world. He must have a rifle, too.

Even though the irony of Kino's desires may escape detection, the ugliness of the world behind paved streets and stone walls does not. And bit by bit its true character also appears to Kino: he is doubtful of the doctor who comes like the Trojan horse, and doubtful of the priest whose blessings in his marriage he had desired. He is cheated and insulted by the pearl buyers, a vocation which he probably had in mind for his son. At this point his education is complete, but he clings to the pearl because his manhood has been challenged by those "dark ones" who attacked him in the night: he knows that "he had lost one world and had not gained another." However, he must go on. Since he has been insulted, he must prove his manhood. It is significant that the Kino who had said that the pearl means a chance for his son is not the same Kino when he leaves the town. Before leaving, Kino says, "I might have given it [the pearl] as a gift . . . but now it is my misfortune . . . I will keep it." Kino's words indicate that he has discarded the illusion of a church marriage and education for Coyotito. In saying that "This pearl has become my soul" Kino has revealed to us that the nature of his struggle and desires has changed; that he is fighting to prove he is a man, and he will not be a "chicken" or cheated. Like Pepé in "Flight," he has defied the social order by cutting himself of from it. The irony, however, is that the reader's real sympathy for him is gained at this point in the novel. From the moment he leaves town we are with him; before this, one's feelings and fears were more like Juana's. But after his hut is burned, and his canoe broken, a point of no return has been created, and only through defiance can Kino attain dignity. Kino knows it and says "Now I will keep it [the pearl]." Giving the pearl up at this point would have meant cowardice; and Kino is a man.

REJECTING DEFEATISM

However, after the trackers are killed and Coyotito is dead, there is no future left for Kino and Juana. Kino returns to town. This return to town and the subsequent throwing of the pearl into the sea has been interpreted as "defeatism" by [critic] Warren French, and *The Pearl* seen as "defective" and "paste." "The time has come," says French, "when Manself will not suffer and die for a concept. Kino suffers, but does not die; and surely if this is 'the pearl of the world,' he is 'Manself.' Having stepped forward painfully, he slips back not just half a step, but toboggans to the very bottom of the heap, for his boat smashed, his baby dead, and the pearl cast into the sea, he has less when the story is over than he had when it started. It is true that he has learned to reject the shoddy material benefits he sought, but there is no indication that he has learned that there might be other alternatives than accepting these or sinking all the way back into his old way of life."

To interpret the throwing of the pearl as defeatism is to miss the point entirely. Kino has suffered, but he has not returned to lie on any bed of roses. For a concept, for the challenge that outraged his manhood, Kino lost his hut, his canoe, and his first born, but Kino is not defeated, nor is he "lazy" as French calls him. He returns to town with the rifle that shot the trackers, "across his arm;" he has returned to town in spite of the four killings. And coming to town was a choice that Kino made. The nature of this choice determines its moral value: he did not come to town to sell the pearl and accept the price the buyers set for it; he did not come to town to say let there be forgiveness, as French interprets it. Kino's return to town indicates that even though everything that a man possesses, including his son, may be lost, yet a man need not be defeated—that those who can suffer for a concept, know how to die for it. The throwing of the pearl does not indicate that Kino has discarded a shoddy materialism; he discarded materialism much earlier in the story. The throwing of the pearl and the return to town are Kino's ultimate defiance of a world that refuses to grant him dignity: his return to town means his death, but in returning to the world Kino attains that dignity which cannot be destroyed or taken away. Kino's return is not only a defiance of the corrupt world, it is a victory of all that is good in man. In the mountains he had become an animal; but by returning to face the world, he becomes larger than life—larger because death cannot be a defeat now. His return is Steinbeck's celebration of that courage in the human heart which no terror can destroy; the people of the town feel his strength, his absolute majesty. In throwing the pearl into the sea, Kino has said that he is still the master of his soul, and will dispose of it the way he likes.

SUPERB WRITING

French also feels that "in manufacturing *The Pearl* Steinbeck seems not to have had his mind on what he wished to say (as in *Cannery Row*), but his eye on what the market would bear." *The Pearl*, in fact, is a superb piece of writing. An examination of the epigraph reveals its meaning. Steinbeck says in the epigraph:

> In the town they tell the story of the great pearl—how it was found and how it was lost again. They tell of Kino, the fisherman, and of his wife, Juana, and of the baby, Coyotito. And because the story has been told so often, it has taken root in every man's mind. And, as with all retold tales that are in people's hearts there are only good and bad things and black and white things and good and evil things and no in-between anywhere.
>
> If this story is a parable, perhaps everyone takes his own meaning from it and reads his own life into it. In any case, they say in the town that . . .

"If this story is a parable, perhaps everyone takes his own meaning from it and reads his own life into it": in these lines there are no antitheses like good or bad, black or white; in these lines we are told that if Kino's life is a parable, then we see our own in it—that life is neither black nor white but a shade in between. Everything in life is relative, and the motive behind one's choice determines the moral value of the act. This is operative in Kino's development in *The Pearl.* Kino is tricked into seeing and wanting things that are not as good as they seem: he feels education brings knowledge and knowledge would set him free; he feels that church makes proper husbands and wives. But as the story progresses he learns that everything is relative. Knowledge of books is good, but only if one is not made to crawl for it; that a church wedding is desirable only if one is not bereft of his manhood in the process. And Kino, like Pepé, learns that manhood is not dependent upon rifles or other trappings. He learns that it is something innate. But once you know that you have it, then you have to fight mountains even if they break you.

A MODEL OF ECONOMY

The Pearl, in fact, is a model of economy. The simple narrative moves like a slow motion picture, but beneath this simplicity is a raging drama that takes place in every man's life—the drama that brings man to choose one line of action than another, even if this choice may mean death and destruction. Kino, in his excitement over the pearl, has a vision of a better life. Having seen this vision, he cannot bring himself to discard it as just illusion; he fights for it. But though in the beginning he was fighting to earn a few personal luxuries, toward the end he is fighting to save this vision. And Kino's movement from personal desires to concepts is not at all different from the Joads' development in *The Grapes of Wrath.* Tom Joad knew he will be killed some day, yet he felt that after death he will be everywhere. "I'll be ever' where you look. Where ever there's a fight so hungry people can eat, I'll be there." Kino knows that he has been ruined, but by throwing the pearl back into the sea he has struck a blow at the foundations on which the exploiter-exploited world of La Paz is built.

The imagery and symbolism, too, have been employed in *The Pearl* with great care. The prey imagery, for example, is highly functional in the novel. In La Paz dogs feed upon fish, and fish on smaller fish, but when men feed upon other men, the same images acquire bad colour, so the author is able to convey a social criticism. Similarly, when Kino acquires the pearl, the pearl is magnificent in its beauty. That beauty is the pearl's beauty—neither evil nor good. It becomes good when Kino projects his own desires into it; the same beauty becomes ulcerous when Kino is made to suffer for the pearl. In this context, what the narrator says about men's minds not being very substantial becomes very significant. Like the haze that hangs over La Paz creating mirages, man's mind plays tricks upon him and makes him see things that are not. The images here help the author in showing the vanity of human wishes and the weakness that all of us carry within. Also the images of darkness and light have been manipulated in such a way that they acquire symbolic meaning. When Kino first awakens it is "near dark": the stars are still in the sky but there is also "a pale wash of light in the lower sky to the east." This atmosphere, neither dark nor light, parallels Kino's state of mind. He is neither happy nor sad: he is content. But after Kino acquires the pearl and has separated himself from everyone because he fears "everyone" Kino "awakened, with the evil music pulsing in him and he lay in the darkness." After Kino has learned that what he wishes is futile, we are told "the dawn was not far off."

Finally, when it is all over, Kino and Juana return to town "late in the golden afternoon" and "the sun was behind them," suggesting the close of Kino's and Juana's lives. Darkness and death go hand in hand in the "stone and plaster" town of La Paz, too. In the doctor's house "the furnishings of the room were heavy and dark," and in the pearl buyer's office "the wooden slats cut out the light."

ANIMAL IMAGERY

As potent as the darkness and light imagery is the animal imagery in the book. A scorpion stings Coyotito, but it is not fatal. More dangerous is the sting of man. The doctor gives the baby "white powder" which could have killed Coyotito had the antidote not been given. The pearl buyer has a "fatherly and benign" face but his eyes are "unwinking as a hawk's eye"; also, the pearl buyer has "many hands" like an insect. Kino "snarls"when he kills the scorpion, and hisses like a "snake" when he beats Juana with "murder in him." Finally, when he knows that it is his life against the others, we are told that Kino "was an animal now, for hiding, for attacking, and he lived only to preserve himself and his family." Highly functional, the animal imagery, like the imagery of darkness, enables the author to impart a non-teleological level to the story's meaning. Man is struggling to stay man, and is capable of being God, yet man falls to the level of animal, destroying others in order to preserve himself.

The symbolism too, is highly effective in *The Pearl*. The major symbol, the pearl, has been inverted. Pearls usually signify purity or innocence which man loses and tries to find. In this novel Kino has innocence and purity which are destroyed after he discovers the pearl. By inverting the symbolism, the writer emphasizes what happens to man when man acquires desires in the shape of a pearl and is made to lose dignity because of it. Steinbeck shows that the desires in the shape of a pearl are not significant; they can be discarded as Ma Joad discards her desire for a white-washed house with oranges growing all around it. But discarding the pearl or the desires need not negate the vision of a future that man has. For that vision Tom Joad and Jim Casy die; for that vision Kino goes to destruction willingly. The pearl then, is a complex symbol: it makes man vulnerable to attack but it makes man stubborn too. And it remains in the people's heart as a possibility—a way of life. This manipulation has allowed the novelist to impart a prophetic level to the story. Man can feed upon man for only so long: Kino and his people have been exploited for four hundred years. They fear, but there is rage and hatred too. And like Kino, they will find the pearl which will make them *create* their future, a future which will shut the door on hunger, and break "the pot that holds" them in. Kino, by coming back to the town, remains the priest of this vision; he emerges as the ideal man—an individual and a group animal.

Steinbeck, then, has not manufactured *The Pearl*. With great care the artist has posed various problems but has not provided any simple answers or scapegoats.

Kino and Juana: The Transformation

Edward E. Waldron

> In his critical reading of *The Pearl*, Edward E. Wal-
> dron focuses on changes that transform Kino and
> Juana into more valuable people, which he exam-
> ines through the metaphor of the pearl. Just as a
> tiny, misplaced grain of sand spurs the process that
> results in a beautiful pearl, so too, social "irritants"
> propel Kino and Juana on a course that, albeit tragic
> on the surface, results in a "pearl without price," the
> couple's newfound relationship of mutual respect.
> The following critical review is excerpted from an
> article Waldron contributed to *Steinbeck Quarterly*, a
> publication dedicated to Steinbeck criticism.

[In] Steinbeck's ending for *The Pearl*, . . . there is a sense of
triumph, horribly muted by the death of Coyotito, in the
strength that brings Kino and Juana back to their village and
allows them to throw the pearl back into the sea. Warren
French finds the ending terribly weak, mainly because of the
"unresolved problems that have been raised by the action"
in the novel. "The conclusion of the novel," he continues,
"leaves the impression that Kino is returning to his old
life. . . ." But are we to conclude that? Is the Kino at the end
of the novel the same Kino who began it? And what of his relationship with Juana? If we read this novel as a positive
work and not as a study in the inevitable defeat of the common man by the pressures of society, then clearly we must
focus on the change that occurs in the characters of Kino
and Juana. Examining those changes through the metaphor
of the pearl gives us another view of what the *real* "pearl of
the world" might be. Early in the novel Steinbeck tells us
how a pearl is formed:

> An accident could happen to these oysters, a grain of sand
> could lie in the folds of muscle and irritate the flesh until in

Excerpted from Edward E. Waldron, "*The Pearl* and *The Old Man and the Sea:* A Com-
parative Analysis," *Steinbeck Quarterly*, Summer/Fall 1980. Reprinted by permission of
the *Steinbeck Quarterly*. Footnotes in the original have been omitted in this reprint.

self-protection the flesh coated the grain with a layer of smooth cement. But once started, the flesh continued to coat the foreign body until it fell free in some tidal flurry or until the oyster was destroyed.

Kino's timely (and melodramatic) discovery of the great pearl after Coyotito is stung by the scorpion can be read as the accident, the "grain of sand," that starts the process. Until that day, Kino had lived his life as his people had always done; the pattern was as predictable as the tides around which their lives were set. The pearl, however, creates visions for Kino, plans that go against the wishes of the gods. But Kino does not draw back from the attack he knows will come:

> To meet the attack, Kino was already making a hard skin for himself against the world. His eyes and his mind probed for danger before it appeared.

The process has begun.

THE TRANSFORMATION BEGINS

Immediately, the first irritant appears as the doctor who was too busy to receive Kino earlier in the day comes out to his hut to see Coyotito. Trapped by his ignorance, Kino must let the doctor work his "magic" on the baby; but when Coyotito gets worse, Kino remembers the white powder, and "his mind was hard and suspicious. . . ." At least in terms of modern American readers, Kino is becoming a more valuable person as he fights to free himself of the twin tyrannies of ignorance and oppression.

Kino is not alone in this transformation. Juana, a good wife and mother, is a strong woman. While she hears Kino's magnificent visions with awe, she nonetheless is ready to defy him and fling the pearl back to the sea when they are attacked and it becomes clear that the pearl represents a threat to her family. After the struggle that leaves one man dead and Kino beaten, it is Juana who finds the pearl by the path. Realizing "that the old life was gone forever," she strengthens Kino's will once more so they may fly from the danger around them. Leaving the village, Juana pads behind Kino. Returning from their ordeal in the wilderness with the lifeless Coyotito slung in her shawl, however, she walks by Kino's side: ". . . they were not walking in single file, Kino ahead and Juana behind as usual, but side by side . . . and they seemed to carry two towers of darkness with them."

The vision of their return recalled by the villagers is one of mystery:

> The people say that the two seemed to be removed from human experience; that they had gone through pain and had come out on the other side; that there was almost a magical protection about them.

The change is also made clear in their actions regarding the pearl. Acknowledging Juana's strength and courage, Kino offers to let her throw the pearl back; she, in turn acknowledging his strength and courage, insists that he throw it. "*They* [my italics] saw the little splash in the distance, and *they* stood side by side watching the place for a long time." Kino and Juana have lost their child, their hut, and their boat, but they have gained something more valuable, a "pearl beyond price," in their new-found relationship of mutual respect. This change may be more important, again, to middle-class American readers than to the Gulf Indians about whom the tale is told, but its impact remains.

Chronology

1902
John Steinbeck born February 27

1903
Wright brothers' airplane flight

1906
San Francisco earthquake and fire

1909
Steinbeck's sister Mary born; Model T Ford first mass produced

1914
World War I begins in Europe; Panama Canal opens

1917
United States enters World War I

1919
Treaty of Versailles ending World War I; Steinbeck graduates from Salinas High School and enters Stanford University

1925
Steinbeck goes to New York, working as a laborer and as a reporter for the *American* newspaper

1927
Charles Lindbergh's first solo transatlantic flight

1928
Talking pictures; first Mickey Mouse cartoon

1929
Stock market crash in America; Hoover becomes president; Steinbeck publishes *Cup of Gold*

1930
Steinbeck marries Carol Henning; meets Edward Ricketts in Pacific Grove, California

1932

America in Great Depression; Charles Lindbergh Jr. kidnapped and murdered; Steinbeck publishes *Pastures of Heaven*

1933

Franklin D. Roosevelt becomes president; Steinbeck publishes *To a God Unknown*

1934

Steinbeck wins O. Henry Prize for "The Murder"; mother dies

1935

Works Progress Administration, work relief for unemployed; Steinbeck publishes *Tortilla Flat*; wins Commonwealth Club of California Gold Medal; Pascal Covici becomes Steinbeck's publisher

1936

Steinbeck publishes *In Dubious Battle*; father dies; publishes articles on migrants in *San Francisco News*

1937

Steinbeck publishes *Of Mice and Men*; Theater Union in San Francisco performs *Of Mice and Men* from the book; stage version performed on Broadway and wins Drama Critics Circle Award; publishes *The Red Pony*, three parts

1938

Steinbeck publishes *The Long Valley* and *Their Blood Is Strong*, a pamphlet based on news articles about migrants

1939

World War II begins in Europe; Steinbeck publishes *The Grapes of Wrath*

1940

Steinbeck and Ricketts's research trip to the Gulf of California, where they gather material for *Sea of Cortez;* while in Mexico, Steinbeck hears a story about a young boy who finds a valuable pearl, an account that he will later fictionalize in *The Pearl;* Steinbeck wins Pulitzer Prize for *The Grapes of Wrath*; films "The Forgotten Village" in Mexico; film versions of *The Grapes of Wrath* and *Of Mice and Men*

1941

Japanese bomb Pearl Harbor; America enters World War II; Steinbeck publishes *The Sea of Cortez* with Ricketts

1942

Steinbeck publishes *The Moon Is Down*; writes script for *Bombs Away;* Steinbeck and Carol Henning divorce; film version of *Tortilla Flat*

1943

Steinbeck marries Gwendolyn Conger; they move to New York; film version of *The Moon Is Down*

1944

D day invasion of Normandy; Steinbeck writes script for *Lifeboat* with Alfred Hitchcock; son Thomas born

1945

Franklin D. Roosevelt dies; Harry Truman becomes president; Americans drop first atomic bomb on Hiroshima; World War II ends; Steinbeck publishes *Cannery Row*; *The Red Pony*, four parts; "The Pearl of the World" in *Woman's Home Companion*

1946

First meeting of the United Nations; son John born

1947

Steinbeck publishes *The Wayward Bus* and *The Pearl*

1948

Berlin blockade and airlift; Steinbeck publishes *A Russian Journal*; elected to American Academy of Letters; film version of *The Pearl*; Edward Ricketts dies; Steinbeck and Gwendolyn Conger divorce

1949

Film version of *The Red Pony*

1950

America involved in Korean War; Steinbeck publishes *Burning Bright*, novel and play; writes script for *Viva Zapata!*; marries Elaine Scott

1951

Steinbeck publishes *The Log from the Sea of Cortez*

1952

Steinbeck publishes *East of Eden*

1953

Dwight D. Eisenhower becomes president

1954

Steinbeck publishes *Sweet Thursday*

1955

Civil rights movement begins; film version of *East of Eden*

1957

Steinbeck publishes *The Short Reign of Pippin IV*; film version of *The Wayward Bus*

1958

Steinbeck publishes *Once There Was a War*

1959

Alaska admitted as forty-ninth state; Hawaii admitted as fiftieth

1960

Steinbeck tours America with dog Charley

1961

John F. Kennedy becomes president; Soviets put up Berlin Wall; first U.S. manned suborbital flight; Steinbeck publishes *The Winter of Our Discontent*

1962

Cuban missile crisis; Steinbeck publishes *Travels with Charley in Search of America*; awarded Nobel Prize in literature

1963

John F. Kennedy assassinated; Lyndon Johnson becomes president

1964–1975

America involved in Vietnam War

1964

Steinbeck awarded the Presidential Medal of Freedom

1965

Steinbeck reports from Vietnam for *Newsday*

1966

Steinbeck publishes *America and Americans*

1968

Martin Luther King Jr. assassinated; televised versions of *Travels with Charley, Of Mice and Men*, and *The Grapes of Wrath*; Steinbeck dies on December 20; buried in Salinas

1969

Richard M. Nixon becomes president; publication of *Journal of a Novel: The* East of Eden *Letters*

1970

Opera version of *Of Mice and Men*

1975

Steinbeck: A Life in Letters, edited by Elaine Steinbeck and Robert Wallstein; publication of *The Acts of King Arthur and His Noble Knights*, Steinbeck's unfinished translation of *Le Morte d'Arthur*

FOR FURTHER RESEARCH

ABOUT JOHN STEINBECK AND *THE PEARL*

Richard Astro, *John Steinbeck and Edward F. Ricketts: The Shaping of a Novelist.* Minneapolis: University of Minnesota Press, 1973.

Richard Astro and Tetsumaro Hayashi, eds., *Steinbeck: The Man and His Work.* Corvallis: Oregon State University Press, 1971.

Jackson Benson, *The True Adventures of John Steinbeck, Writer.* New York: Viking, 1984.

John Ditsky, *John Steinbeck: Life Work, and Criticism.* Fredericton, Canada: York, 1985.

Claudia Durst Johnson, *Understanding* Of Mice and Men, The Red Pony, *and* The Pearl: *A Student Casebook to Issues, Sources, and Historical Documents.* Westport, CT: Greenwood Press, 1997.

Tetsumaro Hayashi, *John Steinbeck: A Dictionary of His Fictional Characters.* Metuchen, NJ: Scarecrow, 1976.

Tetsumaro Hayashi, ed., *A Study Guide to Steinbeck: A Handbook to His Major Works.* Metuchen, NJ: Scarecrow Press, 1974.

Sunita Jain, *John Steinbeck's Concept of Man: A Critical Study of His Novels.* New Delhi: New Statesman, 1979.

Thomas Kiernan, *The Intricate Music: A Biography of John Steinbeck.* Boston: Little, Brown, 1979.

Peter Lisca, *John Steinbeck: Nature and Myth.* New York: Cromwell, 1978.

———, *The Wide World of John Steinbeck.* New Brunswick, NJ: Rutgers University Press, 1958.

Paul McCarthy, *John Steinbeck.* New York: Ungar, 1980.

Lester J. Marks, *Thematic Design in the Novels of John Stein-beck.* The Hague: Mouton, 1969.

Joseph R. Millichap, *Steinbeck and Film.* New York: Ungar, 1983.

Louis Owens, *John Steinbeck's Re-Vision of America.* Athens: University of Georgia Press, 1985.

John C. Pratt, *John Steinbeck.* Grand Rapids, MI: Eerdmans, 1970.

M.R. Satyanarayana, *John Steinbeck: A Study in the Theme of Compassion.* Hyderabad, India: Osmania University Press, 1977.

Elaine Steinbeck and Robert Wallston, eds., *Steinbeck: A Life in Letters.* New York: Viking, 1975.

Ernest W. Tedlock Jr. and C.V. Wicker, *Steinbeck and His Critics: A Record of Twenty-Five Years.* Albuquerque: University of New Mexico Press, 1957.

John H. Timmerman, *John Steinbeck's Fiction: The Aesthetics of the Road Taken.* Norman: University of Oklahoma Press, 1986.

F.W. Watt, *John Steinbeck.* New York: Grove Press, 1962.

HISTORICAL AND LITERARY BACKGROUND

Will Durant and Ariel Durant, *Interpretations of Life: A Survey of Contemporary Literature.* New York: Simon & Schuster, 1970.

Edmund Fuller, *Man in Modern Fiction.* New York: Random House, 1958.

Drewey Wayne Gunn, *American and British Writers in Mexico, 1556–1973.* Austin: University of Texas Press, 1974.

Frederick J. Hoffman, *The Modern Novel in America, 1900–1950.* Chicago: Henry Regnery, 1951.

Harry T. Moore, *Age of the Modern and Other Literary Essays.* Carbondale: Southern Illinois University Press, 1971.

Edith O'Shaughnessy, *Intimate Pages of Mexican History.* New York: George H. Doran, 1920.

B. Ramachandra Rao, *The American Fictional Hero*. Chandigarh, India: Bahri, 1979.

Heinrich Straumann, *American Literature in the Twentieth Century*. 3rd ed. New York: Harper and Row, 1965.

Charles C. Walcutt, *Seven Novelists in the American Naturalist Tradition: An Introduction*. Minneapolis: University of Minnesota Press, 1974.

WORKS BY JOHN STEINBECK

Cup of Gold (1929)

Pastures of Heaven (1932)

To a God Unknown (1933)

Tortilla Flat (1935)

In Dubious Battle (1936)

"The Harvest Gypsies," published in *San Francisco News* (1936)

Saint Katie the Virgin (1936)

Of Mice and Men (1937)

The Red Pony, three parts (1937)

The Long Valley (1938)

Their Blood Is Strong, pamphlet of *San Francisco News* articles (1938)

The Grapes of Wrath (1939)

The Forgotten Village, a film (1940)

Film versions of *The Grapes of Wrath* and *Of Mice and Men* (1940)

The Sea of Cortez, with Edward F. Ricketts (1941)

The Moon Is Down, novel and play (1942)

Bombs Away (1942)

Film version of *Tortilla Flat* (1942)

Film version of *The Moon Is Down* (1943)

Script for *Lifeboat*, a film (1944)

Cannery Row (1945)

The Red Pony, four parts (1945)

"The Pearl of the World" in *Woman's Home Companion* (1945)

The Wayward Bus (1947)

The Pearl (1947)

A Russian Journal (1948)

Film version of *The Pearl* (1948)

Film version of *The Red Pony* (1949)

Burning Bright, novel and play (1950)

Script for *Viva Zapata!*, a film (1950)

The Log from the Sea of Cortez (1951)

East of Eden (1952)

Sweet Thursday (1954)

Pipe Dream, a musical based on *Sweet Thursday* (1955)

Film version of *East of Eden* (1955)

The Short Reign of Pippin IV (1957)

Film version of *The Wayward Bus* (1957)

Once There Was a War (1958)

The Winter of Our Discontent (1961)

Travels with Charley in Search of America (1962)

Newsday columns (1965)

America and Americans (1966)

Television versions of *Travels with Charley, Of Mice and Men*, and *The Grapes of Wrath*; "Here's Where I Belong," a musical (1968)

Journal of a Novel: The East of Eden *Letters* (1969)

Opera version of *Of Mice and Men* (1970)

The Acts of King Arthur and His Noble Knights (1975)

Steinbeck: A Life in Letters, edited by Elaine Steinbeck and Robert Wallstein (1975)

INDEX

Acts of King Arthur and His Noble Knights, The, 26
Astro, Richard, 62

Bakan, David, 30
Baker, Carlos, 77
Bartel, Roland, 95
Benson, Jackson J., 14
Beskow, Bo, 26
Bible, 38, 68, 75, 94, 99
Bombs Away: The Story of a Bomber Team, 24
Burning Bright, 26, 91

California, 21, 22, 27
   Salinas, 13, 15, 27, 111
Cannery Row, 18, 25, 78, 102
   The Pearl a contrast to, 63, 137
   use of musical devices in, 91
characters, 60
   Coyotito, 49, 54, 73, 107, 131
      and close link to pearl, 98-99
      death of, 39, 114, 132
         effect on end of book, 141
         effect on Kino and Juana, 109
      and Kino's return to city, 125
      as sacrifice, 39, 51, 81, 126
      is stung by scorpion, 135, 139, 142
      Kino's hopes for, 70, 81, 117, 119
      as central problem in story, 106-107
      as unconvincing, 106-107
      significance of name, 50, 69, 71, 128
   doctor, 54, 107, 124, 126, 135
      corruption of, 95
      Kino impotent against, 108
      known callousness of, 117-18
      as symbol of degeneration, 61
      as symbol of oppressive class, 60, 98, 127-28
   as withdrawn from people around him, 59
   Juan Tomàs, 36, 76, 85, 104, 127
      as representative of community thinking, 59
      symbolism of name, 50
      theme of survival announced by, 45-46
      understanding of, 44, 120
      pearl buyers, 60, 61, 97, 134, 139
      priest, 70, 96, 106, 124, 134
      pursuers, 78, 96, 127
         facelessness of, 104, 105
         greed of town personified by, 61
      see also Kino; Juana
Chicago Sun Book Week, 92
Conger, Gwendolyn (Steinbeck's second wife), 22, 24
   and divorce, 26
Conrad, Joseph, 49
Covici, Pascal, 20, 30, 90
Cox, Martha Heasley, 122
Cup of Gold, 17

Darwin, Charles, 112
Dissonant Harmony, 19

East of Eden, 26, 105
Esquire (magazine), 18

Fiedler, Leslie A., 129
"Flight," 103, 104, 106, 113, 136
   protagonist of, 102, 105, 110
   symbolism in, 103
Fontenrose, Joseph, 104, 109
Forgotten Village, The, 24
French, Warren, 93, 101, 130, 136, 137

Gladstein, Mimi Reisel, 129
Grapes of Wrath, The, 22, 24, 110, 116, 138

153

Gray, James, 131
Great Depression, the, 18

Habas, Ralph, 92
"Harvest Gypsies, The," 21
Hayashi, Tetsumaro, 48
Heart of Darkness (Conrad), 37
Henning, Carol (Steinbeck's first
    wife), 18, 22, 24

imagery, 33, 40, 47
    animal, 61, 76-78, 86-87, 114,
        139-40
    boat, 60, 82, 130
    duality, 30, 31, 50
    light and dark, 34, 72-73, 103-
        104, 109
    fluctuation of, 30, 75-76
    mountain setting, 76, 102, 105,
        106, 138
        as place of safety, 87
        as unknown, 110
    musical, 31, 36, 46, 54, 124
        as device used in other works,
            91
        duality of, 38, 39
        possible source for, 68, 69
        and Song of the Family, 90
        change in, 81
        inevitability of discord in,
            30, 31
        as symbol of orderly life, 78-
            79
    pearl, as symbol, 64, 68, 106, 140
        of accidental happening, 54,
            142
        combined with other imagery,
            34, 35
        duality of, 32
        and Kino's entrapment, 36,
            38
        formation of, 141-42
        of greed, 48, 73
        is linked to Coyotito, 98-99,
            108
        of soul, 68, 69, 81-82
        was originally positive, 39, 69
    rifle, 93, 98, 106, 109, 136
        as symbol of freedom and
            fear, 82-83
    scorpion, 35, 39, 78, 88, 108
        and Song of the Enemy, 46
        as symbol of evil, 31, 48, 75
Indians, 78, 108, 143

in early twentieth century, 64
    idealized by Ed Ricketts, 63
    in Steinbeck's metaphor, 58
    and Steinbeck's use of mythol-
        ogy, 71-72, 73
In Dubious Battle, 20
irony, 33-34, 109, 132, 135
    of Kino's committing murder
        for a good cause, 39
    of Kino's faith in pearl, 38
    of pearl's development, 32

Jain, Sunita, 134
Johnson, Claudia Durst, 64
Johnson, Lyndon B., 27
*John Steinbeck's Fiction: The Aes-
    thetics of the Road Taken* (Tim-
    merman), 70
Juana, 66, 69, 77, 80, 124
    as ideal woman, 125, 142
    mistrust of pearl by, 36, 37, 50,
        80
    neglected by critics, 130, 131
    significance of, at end of book,
        117
    strength of, 133
    as symbol of endurance, 129
    as symbol of womankind, 131-
        32
    see also characters; Kino and
        Juana
Jung, Carl, 117

Karsten, Ernest E., Jr., 53
Kennedy, John F., 27
Kino, 35, 36, 97
    as animal-like, 86-87, 105, 139
    aspirations of, 33, 43, 45, 135
        as innocent yet fatal, 47
    and separation from commu-
        nity, 48, 54, 55, 59, 65
    compared with Conrad's Kurtz,
        49
    compared with Job, 75
    compared with other Steinbeck
        heroes, 102, 110, 138
    compared with Shakespeare's
        Hamlet, 50
    disillusionment of, 34
    fear of, 76
    isolation of, 104
    and Juana, 69, 88, 89, 117
        changing relationship of, 125-
            26

compared with Adam and
Eve, 29, 31, 37-38, 51, 71
deep feelings of, 99
fight with, 37, 56, 86, 124
innocence of, 134
as parents, 119
as primal pair, 103
reconciliation of, 80
and resemblance to Every-
man, 40
and return to village, 52, 72,
76, 136
as defiant act, 97, 137
as failure to find new life, 98
as mysterious, 143
as new beginning, 61
and new strength, 126, 141
as main protagonist, 83, 89, 95
as member of oppressed community, 64, 85, 98, 108
and rejection of pearl, 63
rise of primitive feelings in, 77,
78
significance of name, 70, 73,
116, 123
struggle of, 66, 81-82, 96, 124
to prove his manhood, 136
stubbornness of, 44
survival demonstrated by, 46
transformation of, 35, 36
as unlikely, 97
as trapped, 107
see also characters
Krause, Sydney J., 101

La Paz, 42, 123, 134, 138, 139
as animal, 87
irony of name, 31-32, 115
language, 84-85, 88, 112
and poetic description, 25, 56-58
positive stress of, 39
see also imagery; structure
Lawrence, D.H., 50
Le Morte Darthur (Malory), 14,
26
Levant, Howard, 107
Lieber, Todd, 36
Lifeboat (movie), 24
Lisca, Peter, 68, 113
Log from the Sea of Cortez, The,
63-64, 104, 106, 112, 113
description of mountain landscape in, 102
and ecology, 41, 42-43
knowledge of Baja history

shown by, 116
as source of story about pearl,
22-25, 41-42, 62, 122-23
themes in, 34, 44-45, 47

Malory, Sir Thomas, 15, 26
Marks, Lester Jay, 38, 130
McIntosh, Mavis, 19
Metzger, Charles R., 41
Meyer, Michael J., 29
Miller, Ted, 17
Millichap, Joseph R., 119
Mirrielees, Edith Ronald, 15
Moon Is Down, The, 24, 91
Morris, Harry, 40, 74, 131
"Murder, The," 20
Murder at Full Moon, 19

Nagle, John M., 84
Newsday, 27
New York American, 17
New York City, 18
New York Herald-Tribune, 24
New York Times Book Review, 77
Nobel Prize, 27
North American Review, 19-20

O'Connor, Richard, 131
Of Mice and Men, 21, 134
original name of, 20
O. Henry Award, 20
Otis, Elizabeth, 19, 20
Owens, Louis, 101

Pastures of Heaven, 19
Pearl, The, 76
as allegory, 68, 73
of evil, 70-71
in part only, 70, 74
of soul, 69
autobiographical aspects of, 41,
119
as parable, 63, 110, 137
author's comment on, 41, 53,
91, 128, 137
of human condition, 66
is too complex, 93-94
reviews of, 26, 92, 101
source for, 92-93, 102, 115, 125
enlarged to include woman
and child, 117, 118, 130
style of, 49, 63, 74, 113
and influence of folklore, 77,
78
various interpretations of, 128

see also characters; *Log from the Sea of Cortez, The;* structure; themes
Pulitzer Prize, 24

Red Pony, The, 19
Ricketts, Ed, 22-23, 104, 111, 123
  death of, 26
  and expedition to Gulf of California, 41-42, 62, 63, 122
  as friend and mentor of Steinbeck, 18, 112
  new titles suggested by, 19, 21

Salinas High School, 15
San Francisco News, 21
satori, 50, 51, 52
Scott, Elaine, 26
Short Reign of Pippin IV, The, 26
Simmonds, Roy, 89
Smith, Stevie, 92
Something That Happened, 20
Sophocles, 51
Spectator, 92
Spreckels Sugar Ranch, 18, 20
Steinbeck, John, 29, 119
  attitude toward *The Pearl*, 94
  childhood of, 13-14
  education of, 15
  personal life of, 18, 19, 22, 26
    and influence on *The Pearl*, 116
  on teleological thought, 43-44, 44-45
  as writer, 17-25
    influence of ecology on, 23, 42-43, 65, 111-12
    and journalist, 21, 24, 27
    and winner of Nobel Prize, 27
  see also Ricketts, Ed
Steinbeck, John Ernst (father), 13, 14, 19, 20
Steinbeck, Mary (sister), 14, 15
Steinbeck, Olive Hamilton (mother), 13, 14, 19
structure, 54, 71, 74, 113-14
  flaws in, 90
    include complexity of moral themes, 93-94
    include unrealistic action, 91
    and proportioning of emphasis, 95-96, 98-99
  simplicity of, 83

and timespan, 72
and use of metaphor, 58-59
and use of symbolism, 74-75
see also imagery; language
Sweet Thursday, 91

Tedlock, E.W., Jr., 111
themes, 52, 54
  community, 59, 120
  vs. town, 32, 56-58, 61, 135
  death of firstborn son, 39
  duality, 33, 34
    ambiguity of possibility, 80
    Kino's misunderstanding of, 35
    need to acknowledge, 38
  gender differences, 116, 126
  hope, 44
    creativity arising from, 45
    and fear, 46-47
    as mutation, 42
    thinking warped by, 43
  moral, 29-30, 40, 70-71
    and Christianity, 68-69, 78
    and Zen philosophy, 49, 50, 51, 52
  survival, 45-46, 87, 132
  see also imagery; irony; *Pearl, The*
Timmerman, John H., 70, 74
To a God Unknown, 19, 102, 105
Tokunaga, Masanori, 111
Tortilla Flat, 19, 20, 24
Travels with Charley in Search of America, 27, 114
Tweedie, Mrs. Alec, 64
Understanding Of Mice and Men, The Red Pony *and* The Pearl (Johnson), 64

Viva Zapata!, 26

Wagner-Martin, Linda, 115
Waldron, Edward E., 141
Wayward Bus, The, 26, 70
Wicker, C.V., 111
Wilhelmson, Carl, 19
Wilson, Edmund, 114
Winter of Our Discontent, The, 27
Woman's Home Companion, 25, 134

Zen philosophy, 49, 50, 51, 52